How will humans around the world live?
Azadi Se Zindagi (Come Know)

The voice of people all over the world.

AUTHOR

Meghraj Singh Khalsa

Published by: Voice of Humanity News Channel, America

Type Setting: Aman Ali Qureshi

Printed in the United States of America

How will humans all over the world live a life of freedom (let's know)

Author: Meghraj Raj Singh Khalasa (American)

First instance -: 18-June-2022

Publisher: Voice of Humanity News Channel, America

Contribution amount: Rs 100/=

Type Setting: Aman Ali Qureshi

TO GET THE BOOK PLEASE CONTACT

House No.: - 6503, Second Floor, Gali Hanuman Mandir, Nabi Karim, Paharganj, New Delhi - 110055, (Landmark) - Rajdhani Hospital, Baburam So Lanki Marg, Sarveshwarve Kumar - 7550666503

Main Topics of the Book

- What are the types of slavery and what is its solution?
- Important, amazing and mysterious information related to mind.
- Important, wonderful and mysterious things related to the mind
- Good Message
- Role
- What are the types of slavery, and what is its solution?
- Poetry
- After death, some will go to heaven and some will go to hell.
- This is all imaginary thought.
- Poetry: Attacks on innocents are illegitimate.
- Poetry: Do not befriend a false person
- Poetry: Make friendship with a true person
- Poem: The path of lies is painful
- Poem: The path of truth is pleasant
- Poem: Truth is like nectar for man, lie is like poison for man
- Thoughts
- About the Author Media and Social Media

What are the types of slavery and what is its solution?

1. Friend, are people all over the world living a life of freedom? (14)

2. Friend, what kind of answer have you given? When we look carefully inside the whole world, we see people all over the world very happy and almost everyone has There been houses, cars, money, having all this, how can a person become a slave?........(14)

3. Friend, on what basis are you saying that almost 98% of the people in the world What proof do you have that they are living a life of slavery (14)

4. Well, if you consider yourself to have experienced knowledge, then tell us with your experienced knowledge that how many types of slavery are spread in the world, and how can we identify this slavery? Let us see today your experienced knowledge. What does it say about slavery? (15)

5. Friend, you have told me so much about slavery that I understand. It is a matter   outside of this, tell us in detail about this slavery? (15)

6. Friend, you have first written about religious slavery. How can there be religious slavery? Religious things are related to religion. Explain clearly how religious slavery can happen? (16)

7. Friend, how can there be slavery in the name of religion? Religion shows the right path to man, then how can we accept slavery in the name of religion? ....(16)

8. Friend, explain a little clearly about slavery of the body. Although everyone knows about the slavery of the body, still if you want to tell something, then tell me? (17)

9. Friend, what is mental slavery and how do we identify it?........(18)

10. Friends, what do you call traditional slavery? (19)

11. Friend, can you tell us about civilizational slavery? (19)

12. Friend, how can culture be slavery? Culture is a human being's culture teaches us that we cannot consider it as slavery. Explain this a little clearly? (19)

13. Friend, what would you like to say about the slavery of racism? In my opinion, racism cannot be slavery because we call it racism as if it is a common thing to have people of different colors in the whole world, we cannot call it slavery of racism? (20)

14. Friend, how can there be slavery based on caste? Caste is a part of Hindu religion; how can we consider it slavery? (21)

15. Friend, your statement that the caste system is slavery is 100% false. The caste system is the four pillars of Hinduism on which the palace of Hinduism

is built. How can the system of four varnas of Hinduism be a slave? You should stop lying and writing? (21)

16. Friend, explain in detail the slavery of ignorance? (22)

17. Friend, how can there be slavery to knowledge? You are also telling strange names of slavery; in this way you are trying to consider yourself very clever and clever. Knowledge means knowledgeable. How can a knowledgeable person become a slave? ... (23)

18. Friend, what does slavery of ego mean? Explain clearly about slavery of ego. We have heard for the first time that there is slavery of ego also. How can a person come out of this? .(24)

19. Friend, do you consider hatred also as slavery? Hate is man's life If hatred is slavery, then how can humans protect themselves from it. Can? (25)

20. Friend, is there slavery of beauty, looks or even job? All this is a gift of nature, can't we call it slavery? (26)

21. Friend, how can there be slavery of colors? Color is a minor thing in front of humans. If there can be slavery of colors, then how will humans be saved from it? (27)

22. Friend, this is the first time we have heard about slavery of clothes. You are describing such slavery, which has no head and no legs. What you are saying is complete nonsense. Clothes are only used to cover

the body. How can clothe covering the body be slavery? ... (27)

23. Friend, it is very difficult for us to understand the slavery of greed but looking at your appearance, it does not seem that you can give correct information about the slavery of greed, yet you explain the slavery of greed in detail, and how can a person escape from the slavery of greed? (28)

24. Friend, we cannot call the slavery of high and low as slavery because high and low is a part of Hindu religion, we will not consider it as slavery, you prove it as slavery and if it is slavery then how will the human being come out of this slavery?... ... (29)

25. Friend, what is inferiority complex? Why have you called inferiority complex as slavery and if inferiority complex is slavery, then how can a human being come out of it? (31)

26. Friends, those who consider themselves special (capable) are also slaves. Can you please explain this? ....(32)

27. Friend, how can we recognize the slavery of the mind and how can a person get out of the slavery of the mind? (33)

28. Friend, you have talked about the slavery of mind. If a person's mind gets spoiled then also talk about what harm does the spoiled mind cause? (36)

29. Friend, you have started talking about very wise and thoughtful things. Okay, let's ask one more question,

why is hatred spreading in the whole world? I see how knowledgeable you are considering yourself to be, let us also see whether your knowledge is right or wrong?... (38)

30. Friends, if we look carefully around the world, there are many religions in the whole world, there are many religious places and those propagating religion will be in millions, not millions. Friends, explain clearly why despite so many religions, so many religious places and so many preachers, they could not eliminate hatred from within the whole world, what are the reasons behind this? (39)

31. Friend, you get scared after seeing the question, no question is dangerous, you have already answered this question. Friend, my next question is that among women and men all over the world, who is mentally stronger, woman or man? Please clarify about this? (42)

32. Friend, after listening to you, it seems that you have a lot of knowledge about religion. A question arises again and again in my mind that the amount of blood that is being shed in the world due to religious fanaticism is not equal to the amount of blood that has been shed in the world's wars and conflicts and this question is not only in my mind but in the minds of crores of people. And I think this question is very difficult for you but I want 100% answer to this question?...... (44)

33. Friend, when did I say that I am a religious person? I am just trying to ask you questions on the issue of religion. Come on, leave aside the issue of whether I am religious or irreligious. You answer me the next question like you answered the previous question. In the answer, it has been said that blood has not been shed because of religious fanaticism, but because of irreligious fanaticism, blood has been shed all over the world. Now tell me, who spread this irreligious fanaticism in the entire world, and who are the people behind it? .... (46)

34. Friend, you talk very big, but you do not have even a single penny of experience and knowledge. You have given the answer to my question absolutely nonsense. How can Brahmins and Jews be mental slaves? Brahmins and Jews are ruling the entire world. How can those who rule be mental slaves? (47)

Important, amazing and mysterious information related to mind.

35. Friends, how should women all over the world use their mental strength properly? (48)

36. Friends, how should men all over the world use their mental strength properly? (49)

37. Friends, all religious people do religious activities so that their mind becomes calm and many religious people also say that I am doing religious activities for peace of mind, or I am doing religious activities for peace of mind. I am a friend, how to identify whether the mind of those doing religious work has become peaceful or not? ... (50)

38. Friend, if the mind becomes calm after doing religious work or any good work, then how should we identify it? (52)

39. Friend, sometimes our mind gives us a lot of happiness, and sometimes it gives us a lot of sorrow. What is the reason behind this? Tell us clearly why the mind does this? (54)

40. Friends, children should improve their mind, youth should improve their mind, women should improve their mind and elders and all other people should know an easy way to improve their mind. Tell (56)

41. Some important, amazing poetry. (58)

Important, wonderful and mysterious things related to the mind

42. Question-41. Friend, which is the right way to live life and how many types of paths are people living all over the world following? (59)

43. Question-42. Friend, if we have knowledge, then should we teach that knowledge to others or not? If we should teach it, then what can be the thinking of the people of the whole world about it? Tell us in some detail? (60)

44. Question-43. Friends, all over the world, almost 95% of the children between the age of 13 to 19 years are the ones who act as per their wish. Many times, the children of this age speak very badly about their parents. Friend, what should the children of this age do? By which They remained safe from mental slavery throughout their life and their parents also remained happy with their children? (61)

45. Question-44. Friend, there is a conscious power in the human mind. How can a person awaken that power and reveal a little about which people have awakened conscious power? (63)

46. Question-46. Friend, there is a population of approximately 7.5 billion people in the entire world. None of them have had the darshan of God till date. Explain clearly what is the reason behind this? (65)

47. Question-46. Friend, there is a population of approximately 7.5 billion people in the entire world. None of them have had the darshan of God till date. Explain clearly what is the reason behind this? (67)

48. Question-47. Friend, many people have this question that why have we come into this world, or why has God sent us to this earth or have we come into this world just to have fun? What is your opinion about this question? (70)

49. Question-48. Friends, what are the things people around the world think that cause harm to themselves mentally and physically? (73)

50. Question-49. Friends, what do people around the world think about that benefit themselves mentally and physically? (74)

51. Question-50. Friend, who do you consider to be the most powerful person in the world? (75)

52. Question-51. Friend, this question arises again and again in the minds of many people that they should clarify a little about whom they should make as their role model? ... (76)

53. Question-52. Friend, you must be aware that people all over the world are afraid of the name of hell and hell and run after the greed of heaven and heaven. Friend, tell us in detail about where is hell and hell, and where is heaven and heaven? (77)

54. Question-53. Friend, we all have five disorders within us. Tell us a little about the advantages and disadvantages of the five disorders so that we can learn some wisdom. (79)

55. Question-54. Friend, if there is any kind of fear inside a person, then what is the benefit, and what is the harm to the person from fear? (82)

56. Question-55. Friend, you talk very big about humanitarianism and also try to call the people of

the whole world as your family members. What work have you done to show the people of the world the path of truth, which will help the whole world? Can people live a life of peace and brotherhood by following the path of truth? (83)

57. Question-56. Friends, why do wars take place within the world and how can wars be ended within the world? (86)

58. Poetry, avoid being friends with wrong person (90).

59. Poetry, make friendship with a true person... (91)

60. Poetry, the path of lies is painful. ... (92)

61. Poetry, the path of truth is happiness (93)

62. Some special important and amazing information... (94)

63. What have we learned from the truth.... (95)

64. Poetry is like nectar for true human beings. ... (96)

65. Note... (98)

66. Idea (98)

67. About the author Media and social media. (107)

Good Message

My name is Dr. Kripal Singh, and I am from Detona Beach, Florida, USA. I have been in America for almost 50 years. Most of the people in the world are busy in their own work like in their business and many people keep running after greed, but some people collect more and more wealth to keep themselves happy and some people keep running after dishonesty, some people are happy due to personal issues, some people are troubled by diseases but when I see Meghraj Singh, he is happy and satisfied, despite being so busy, he works 15 hours a day and is also running a TV channel. Meghraj Singh has written a wonderful book named "How humans of the whole world will live a free life" with the help of double truth. This book is very beneficial for the people of the whole world and whoever reads this book will be free from mental slavery. And in this he has discussed many forms of slavery. This book provides information about how many types of slavery are there and by reading this book any person can come out of slavery and after reading this book, how to come out of slavery and how to live a life of freedom, this is written very well in this book. Is., I congratulate Meghraj Singh for this amazing work and recommend you all to read this book and practice the suggestions given to be successful in your life as well as to help others. My best wishes are with all of you and I appreciate Meghraj Singh for writing this book. Thank you so much...

Dr. Kripal Singh (M.D.)

Role

Respected dear friends -

The thoughts about this book that you are going to read were running in my mind continuously for two years. I was wondering how many types of slavery there are in the whole world and how can people all over the world be free from this slavery.

Two years ago, I was going to New York sitting in a taxi. When we entered New York City, I was thinking about this book, then the taxi driver started asking me, Sir, what are you thinking. So, I told him that I am thinking of writing a book on how many types of slavery are there in the whole world. Then the driver looked back at me and said, "You seem simple and innocent, and you are talking very big things. Saying this he smiled a little and When I started driving, these thoughts were going through my mind. At that time, only one book of mine had come in the market named (Are Sikhs Hindus, know the truth). After that I wrote two more books whose names are as follows:

1. Are Sikhs Hindus, know what is the truth

2. Truth is the only religion.

3. Let us know what is the right solution to the serious problem of families and the world.

In these three books we have given questions and answers, similarly in this fourth book also we have given questions and answers. In this book, we have shown two friends answering questions. We have changed the name of this book to (How many types of slavery are there in the world) and have named this book (Come know how people of the whole world will live with freedom). In this book, we have talked about how many types of slavery are there in the world and how a person can live a happy life by becoming free from that slavery. This is the way we have shown in this book.

I request all of you to read this book carefully because reading it carefully will benefit you a lot. Those who will read this book carefully will free themselves from slavery and will also be able to free people from slavery.

You all have blessed me with love by reading my first three books.

After reading this fourth book, you will again be enriched with love and you yourself will also become enriched with knowledge. My best wishes are with you all.

Yours,

Meghraj Singh Khalsa
(America)

What are the types of slavery, and what is its solution?

Question 1. Friends, are people all over the world living a free life?

Answer: No, dear friend, there are only about one or two percent of people in the whole world who are living a life of freedom and the rest are living a life of slavery.

Question 2. Friend, what kind of answer have you given? When we look carefully inside the entire world, we see people all over the world very happy and almost everyone has houses, cars, money, having all this, how can a person be a slave?

Answer-Dear friend, having houses, cars, money is one thing and being a slave is a different thing. Many times, we have seen that even those who have houses, cars and money remain trapped in slavery. They are not even aware that they are trapped in slavery. I believe that despite having money, car, house, almost 98% people can be slaves.

Question 3. Friend, on what basis are you saying that almost 98% of the people in the world are living a life of slavery? What proof do you have for this?

Answer-Dear friend, if you look carefully inside the whole world, you will come to know that almost 98% of the people in the whole world are trapped in slavery. I am explaining to you by giving an example. such as -

- There are many countries fighting among themselves all over the world.

- States are fighting each other.

- Fighting is taking place inside cities and villages.

- Fighting is taking place in every home.

- Most of the people are living life in worries, anger and hatred.

These five examples we have given are all signs of mental slavery and as far as proof is concerned, I have tried to understand it with experienced knowledge. There is no proof of experienced knowledge. This experienced knowledge is the knowledge of nature, which a person can understand only by following the path of truth and honesty. Could.

Question-4. Well, if you consider yourself to have experienced knowledge, then tell me with your experienced knowledge that how many types of slavery are spread in the world, and how can we identify this slavery? Let us see today what you experienced knowledge says about slavery?

Answer - Dear friend, according to my personal experience, the following types of slavery are spread all over the world **such as -**

1. Religious slavery
2. Slavery in the name of religion
3. Slavery of the body
4. Mental slavery
5. Traditional slavery

6. Civilizational slavery
7. Cultural slavery
8. Slavery to racism
9. Slavery of caste
10. Caste slavery
11. Slavery of ignorance
12. Slavery of knowledge
13. Slavery to ego and pride
14. Slavery to Hate
15. Slavery to beauty
16. Slavery to colors
17. Slavery to clothes
18. Slavery to greed
19. Slavery of high and low
20. Slavery of inferiority complex
21. Slavery of considering oneself special
22. Slavery of the mind

Question-5. Friend, you have told so much about slavery, it is beyond my understanding, tell me in detail about this slavery?

Answer - Dear friend, you can ask one by one about the slavery you want to know about in detail.

Question-6. Friend, you are the first to write about religious slavery. How can religious slavery happen? Religious things are related to religion. Please explain clearly how religious slavery can happen?

Answer - Dear friend, you are right in saying that religious matters are related to religion. Understanding the issue of religion is not as easy as you think. The issue of religion is very big. Religious matters can be understood only by following the path of truth and honesty. Accepting religious matters without thinking is religious slavery. The sign is that those who have lies and dishonesty in them cannot understand the things of religion, and those who blindly believe in the things of religion are also trapped in religious slavery. If we are hating and lying to others in the name of religion, then we are committing religious slavery.

I am trapped. In the name of religion, if we are loving others and speaking the truth, then we are not trapped in religious slavery.

Question-7. Friend, how can there be slavery in the name of religion? Religion shows the right path to man, then how can we accept slavery in the name of religion?

Answer-Dear friend, slavery in the name of religion means that whatever we hear or read in the name of religion, accepting it as 100% truth is a sign of slavery to religion. Nowadays, there is a lot of confusion in the name of religion. In the name of religion, man has become so fanatic that he is not ready to listen against his own religion and every person of every religion is promoting his own religion as bigger. Whether his words are false or true, every person has his own opinion. He or she makes the matter bigger. In the name of religion, man has become so weak that he tortures the poor and also considers himself religious. Killing the poor in the name of religion, and harassing people of other religions is slavery in the name of religion. Helping the poor in the name of religion and discussing ideas with people of other religions is freedom in the name of religion.

Question-8. Friend, please explain a little clearly about the slavery of the body. Although everyone knows the slavery of the body, still if you want to tell something then please tell?

Answer-Dear friend, let me try to explain about the slavery of the body by giving some examples such as -

1. Keeping innocent people in jail.

2. Trying to prove innocent people guilty.

3. Torturing innocents in or out of jails.

4. To unnecessarily show off your inferiority complex to an officer.

5. Flattering superior officers.

6. To show unnecessary dominance over your wife.

7. Don't believe even the right words of your own people.

8. Forcing your children to do wrong things also.

9. Getting work done by others without money.

10. Misusing your power.

All these are examples of physical slavery. Only an ignorant person will enslave himself and others to the body. Only a knowledgeable person will free himself and others from the slavery of the body.

Question-9. Friend, what is mental slavery, and how can we identify it?

Answer: Dear friend, mental slavery is more dangerous than physical slavery. Because this slavery is not visible to the eyes. This mental slavery can be seen only through the eyes of knowledge. Very few people in the whole world know about the eyes of knowledge. I will try to explain you about mental slavery by giving examples such as -

1. Those who are themselves trapped in mental slavery are the ones who try to enslave others too.

2. Remain afraid of within in the name of hell and hell.

3. To give charity to others in the name of heaven and heaven.

4. To worship your Lord, Waheguhe Ru, Allah, without any fear.

5. Do not obey your God, God, Allah, Waheguhe Ru because of any greed.

6. Accepting the words of any knowledgeable person without thinking.

7. Reject the words of any ignorant person without thinking.

8. Accepting the words of any scripture without thinking.

9. Donating to Brahmins or any religious people in the name of your dead elders.

10. Shedding the blood of innocent people and innocent people of other religions in the name of religion, etc., all these are examples of mental slavery. This is my personal experience. Someone else's experience may be more or less than these examples. If there is even one of these examples in a person, then he is trapped in mental slavery. Man can identify himself by reading these examples.

If any person in the world has lies and dishonesty in his mind, he will remain trapped in mental slavery. If any person in the world adopts truth and honesty, he will be free from mental slavery.

Question-10. Friends, what is traditional slavery?

Answer - Dear friend, traditional slavery is called that which our ancestors have been doing or the work which we have been doing in the name of religion. If we have been doing that work without thinking, or we have been doing the work of that religion without paying attention, then we are trapped in traditional slavery. If we follow old things without thinking, we will not be able to recognize right and wrong. When we will not recognize right and wrong, we will never be able to get out of traditional slavery. If we think carefully and believe in old or new things, then only we will know what is right and wrong.

Will be able to identify. Only people who can distinguish between right and wrong can live a life of freedom forever.

Question-11. Friend, can you tell us about civilizational slavery?

Answer - Dear friend, nowadays in the name of civility, many things are shown which seem like a slander on the name of civility. If we close our eyes and accept it as truth, it would mean that we have not used our brain properly. People who use their brain properly never accept anything without reasoning. People who reason do not fall into any kind of slavery. People who speak the truth can recognize civilized slavery.

Question-12. Friend, how can there be slavery in culture? Culture teaches man values.

We cannot consider culture as slavery, explain this a little clearly?

Answer - Dear friends, you must have heard, and we have also heard that this culture is thousands of years old, which our elders have been continuously believing in. Very few people would know about who was behind the culture or when the culture has been coming since and most of the people would know about the culture. They don't even want to, they say that the work done by our elders cannot be wrong, they don't even once use their brain to find out who taught this culture to our elders or who used this culture as a means to teach values. Whether the culture is old or new, it should not be followed without thinking.

Question-13. Friend, what would you like to say about the slavery of racism? In my opinion, racism cannot be slavery because we call it racism as if it is

a common thing to have people of different colors all over the world. We cannot call it slavery or racism.

Answer - Dear friend, the problem of racism is a big problem for all of us, do not consider it so easy. Racism is a dangerous mental illness born from ignorance which causes less harm to others and causes more harm to oneself. Is such as -

1. This is fair, this is black, this is brown, all are different, this is inferior to me.

2. Thinking like this will create hatred inside a person.

3. When there is hatred inside, then he will think wrong about others.

4. When the mind thinks wrong, then a person will also do wrong.

5. When a person does wrong, then others will also do wrong after seeing him.

6. When a person himself does wrong, he will make others do wrong too.

7. When he himself makes others do wrong, then he can also go to jail.

8. When a person does wrong, then racism will arise in him.

9. When there is racism inside him then he will lose his peace, tolerance and his good qualities.

10. He will waste his most precious time due to racism.

Question-14. Friend, how can there be slavery based on caste? If caste is a part of Hindu religion, how can we consider it slavery?

Answer: Dear friend, caste-based slavery is a part of mental slavery. It is mental slavery. We call that slavery which we are not aware of and in that slavery, we are considering ourselves free, or we are considering it as our fate. Casteism is such a terrible mental slavery that creates discrimination and hatred among humans due to which man gets away from his real life. Truth will never survive in a person trapped in the mental slavery of caste. Truth cannot survive where there is inferiority complex and pride. Those whom people call low caste develop an inferiority complex, and those whom people call high caste develop pride in them. In a society where there is casteism, truth will not prevail. In a society where there is no truth, that society cannot be religious, that is why we can call casteism as slavery, slavery can never be a part of any religion. Only if we speak the truth and listen to the truth will we be able to understand the slavery of caste. By the true mercy of the true God, we will be saved from the slavery of inferiority complex and pride

Question-15. Friend, what you have said about the caste system as slavery is 100% false. The caste system is the four pillars of Hindu religion on which the palace of Hindu religion is built. How can the system of four castes of Hindu religion be a slave? Do you stop lying and writing?

Answer - Dear friend, caste system is slavery, we will prove it to be slavery and what you are saying to us is 100% false, and you have described four varnas as four pillars and Hindu religion as a palace made of four pillars, and you are telling us that We are saying that we should stop lying and writing. Dear friend, whether you consider our words as a hundred percent false or one lakh percent false, this cannot make our true words false, and you are saying that there are four varnas, which are the four pillars on which the palace of Hindu religion is built, this is absolutely wrong because there are four varnas. Varnas means four parts of one religion and four parts means four pieces and these pieces mean using one power at four places. When we use one power at four places then we will not get success in any field. When we do not get success, then in A dilemma arises as to why we do not get success. Due to the four varnas, there was a dilemma among the humans and due to the dilemma, there was hatred among the varnas. Due to hatred, the humans lost truth, honesty and humanity.

Lost. A religion which does not have true honesty and humanity cannot be a religion, it can only be called slavery and if you find my written truth to be a lie then it is not your fault because you have never heard the truth nor have you ever read the truth. . Hey dear friend, I am crazy about the truth, I will keep writing the truth and speaking the truth no matter what the people of the world think about me.

Whoever believes in the caste system as religion will never be able to come out of slavery. The one who

abandons the caste system will come out of slavery forever.

Question-16. Friend, explain in detail the slavery of ignorance?

Answer - Dear friend, very few people know about the slavery of ignorance. Uneducated people are less trapped in this slavery and educated people are very much trapped in this slavery. Only those who are truthful and honest can talk about this slavery.

One who does not have truth in his mind, whether he is educated or illiterate, both will remain trapped in the slavery of ignorance. Only those who have truth in their mind will be able to live out of the slavery of ignorance.

Question-17. Friend, how can there be slavery of knowledge? You are also giving strange names of slavery; in this way you are trying to consider yourself very clever and clever. Knowledge means knowledgeable. How can a knowledgeable person be a slave?

Answer - Dear friend, it is an easy thing to get out of the slavery of ignorance but it is not an easy thing to get out of the slavery of knowledge. The first thing is that no one considers knowledge as slavery. The second thing is that when a person does not consider knowledge as slavery. If you understand then how will you get out? Dear friend, I am telling you the following reasons due to which a person gets trapped in the slavery of knowledge such as -

- He texts from which one is learning knowledge are to be considered as the final texts of knowledge.

- After learning knowledge, consider yourself fully knowledgeable.

- Have a feeling of defeating others while discussing knowledge.

- Insulting others while discussing knowledge.

- Considering others as fools on the basis of knowledge.

- To be proud of one's knowledge.

- Consider the learned knowledge as your personal knowledge.

- Do not teach the learned knowledge to others.

- Spreading hatred among people with your knowledge.

- Do not consider anyone more knowledgeable than yourself.

Dear friends, these 10 examples that we have given are the actions of those who consider themselves knowledgeable. According to my personal experience, I consider this to be slavery of knowledge and you are telling me that I am trying to consider myself clever and clever, then friend, you may think so about me but this is not the reality. The reality is that I am a student learning knowledge. This is how I, my friend, can identify the slavery of knowledge. If we consider ourselves knowledgeable and great, then we are in slavery to knowledge. If, despite being knowledgeable, we consider ourselves to be an ordinary human being, then we are not in slavery to knowledge.

Question-18. Friend, what is the meaning of slavery of ego and ego? Explain clearly about the slavery of ego and ego. We have heard for the first time that there is slavery of ego and ego also. How can a person come out of this?

Answer - Dear friend, very few people have written about the slavery of ego and mind and most of the people do not even know about the slavery of ego and do not even believe. Dear friend, the second name of ego is pride. If a person has too much pride in money, gold-silver, diamonds-jewels, land-property, etc., then pride stops the development of a person's intelligence.

The one whose intelligence stops developing is called arrogant and boastful. Many times, such people do a lot of harm to themselves due to ego and then repent later, still they do not leave the ego or do not come out of the slavery of ego. If he reads the poetry given below carefully, he will be freed from slavery.

Those people who get attached to anything, whether it is money, gold, silver or earth, considering it as their own, they will remain in the bondage of egoism.

The person who does not get attached to money, gold, silver or gold by considering it as his own, will remain free from the slavery of egoism.

Question-19. Friend, do you consider hatred also as slavery? Hate is a part of human life. If hatred is slavery, then how can man protect himself from it?

Answer - Dear friend, hatred is also a slavery. Hate is spread almost all over the world due to which man is causing harm to himself, his family, society and the whole world. People can guess from this that in what ways hatred is causing harm. Whatever harm is caused to a person's life, we can call it slavery of hatred. Due to hatred, we ourselves keep burning in the fire of hatred. Due to hatred, man causes a lot of harm to himself. Such as -

- If we hate others our attention will shift towards others.

- When there is hatred within us then evil will arise within us.

- When there are evils within us then good people will go away from us.

- When good people are not together then people will turn to crime.

- When a person commits a crime, he will either go to jail or be killed

All these losses are caused by hatred. Dear friend, I am telling you through poetry how a person can save himself from the slavery of hatred. Such as

If you make friendship with true people, you will be saved from hatred.

By learning the qualities of honest people, you will become virtuous yourself.

You will be saved from hatred if you make friendship with true people.

You will become virtuous yourself by learning the virtues of honest people.

You will be able to win the hearts of your loved ones and the society with your good qualities.

By acquiring good qualities, you will find happiness within yourself.

When there is happiness within then hatred will disappear from within.

As soon as hatred disappears, there will be happiness all around in life.

Only because of truth the slavery of hatred will end.

Meghraj Singh: True people will see the world again.

Question-20. Friend, is there slavery of beauty, looks or even job? All this is a gift of nature, can't we call it slavery?

Answer - Dear friend, there is slavery of beauty or we can also call it slavery of looks or body. Dear friend, a person realizes his beauty, looks or appearance only after about 16 years of age. If any person is proud of his beauty, looks or appearance and considers others to be less beautiful, looks or appearance than him. If you believe then a person will be trapped in the slavery of beauty, looks and job. You are 100% right that beauty, looks and body are gifts of nature, but whatever nature gives, it also takes back. The beauty, the looks, the beauty that comes goes away and never comes back. It would be foolish to be proud of the things that come and go.

Only foolish people get trapped in slavery and due to this slavery, man leaves his peaceful life and reaches a life of sorrows. Then he dies after spending his whole life in sorrow. Man can come out of this slavery of beauty, appearance and job in such a way as

If a person takes pride in his beauty, looks and what he has become, then

Will remain trapped in slavery.

If a person does not take pride in his beauty, looks and what he has become, then he

Will be able to live life freely.

-

Question-21. Friend, how can there be slavery of colors? Color is a simple thing in front of humans. If there can be slavery of colors then how will humans be saved from it?

Answer - Dear friend, slavery is everywhere in this world. There should be a human perspective to recognize slavery. Dear friend, there are many types of colors in this world and there are many religions, almost all the religions have different colors such as -

1. Someone's saffron, someone's green, someone's white, someone's yellow, someone's spring,

someone's blue, all these colors have been adopted by people of almost different religions.

2. Dear friend, there are all the religions in the world. If the people of those religions are intelligent then they will respect the colors of all the religions. If the people of those religions are ignorant then they will insult the colors of other religions. Only those people who are trapped in slavery insult. We can become free from the slavery of colors of religion in such a way as -

If people continue to hate the colors of other religions, they will remain trapped in slavery. If people love the colors of all religions, then they will be free from slavery.

Question-22. Friend, we have heard about the slavery of clothes for the first time. You are describing such a slavery which has no head and no legs. What you are saying is complete nonsense. Clothes are only used to cover the body. How can clothes covering the body be slavery?

Answer - Dear friend, you are right that clothes are used to cover the body, this is fine, but as long as the clothes are used to cover the body, as per the wish of the people, then it is fine, but when the clothes are forced to be worn by someone else. If so, then it becomes the cause of slavery. To force someone to do any work or to make someone do it, both are slavery. If you are forcing someone to wear clothes or are forcing someone to wear clothes, then come out of it because slavery traps the human mind in mental slavery.

Question-23. Friend, it is very difficult for us to understand the slavery of greed but looking at your face it does not seem that you can give correct information about the slavery of greed, still you explain the slavery of greed in detail and how can a person escape from the slavery of greed?

Answer - Dear friend, greed is so dangerous in a person's life that it ruins everything, happiness and peace in a person's life. Greed gives rise to many of the following weaknesses such as - dishonesty, corruption, misconduct, rapist, devil's destiny, evil is destiny. , pride, inferiority complex. All these weaknesses arise from slavery to greed. A person trapped in the slavery of greed always remains troubled. If a person is greedy then his mind will not be satisfied even after having everything at home. If greed becomes big then it can take away the entire world's wealth, gold, silver, diamonds and jewels.

Even if he gets it he is not satisfied. A person trapped in the slavery of greed keeps wandering all the time. To satisfy greed, many times a person commits big crimes and then goes on saving his life. Dear friend, a person can come out of the slavery of greed in such a way as -

- Greed is very bad which eats away the happiness of a person.

- Despite having money, gold and silver, a person can become poor.

- Sometimes greed also makes a person commit crimes.

- Then that greed even gets a person hanged because of the crime.

- A person trapped in greed may even become the richest person in the entire world.

- Because of greed that person could not live a single day in peace.

- They do not find happiness anywhere even if they roam around in all directions.

- Sometimes at home and sometimes outside, greed made them stray a lot.

- Whoever accepts the truth wholeheartedly, may the truth save him from greed.

- A person should not be distracted by the sight of gold, silver, rupees, diamonds and jewels.

- Good qualities are born from truth through which patience and satisfaction can be found.

- With patience and satisfaction, all the weaknesses within a person can be removed.

- The one whose greed has ended will see mud and gold as equal.

- May all his sorrows, sorrows and worries end on the path of truth.

- The true knowledge of great men should light the lamp of knowledge within man.

- By the grace of Meghraj Singh Guru, a true person can once again find ultimate happiness.

Question-24. Friend, we cannot call the slavery of high and low as slavery because high and low is a part of Hindu religion, we will not consider it as slavery, you prove it as slavery and if it is slavery then how will man come out of this slavery?

Answer - Dear friend, on what basis are you saying that there cannot be high-low slavery? I will prove to you that high-low slavery only exists. Dear friend, the issue of slavery between high and low is related to the mind. If the mind of a person truly embraces knowledge, then the mind makes the person knowledgeable. If the mind is trapped in ignorance, then the mind makes the person a great fool and a devil. Dear friend, what does a person trapped in ignorance think about others? Is such as -

- This black is below me and the white one is above me.

- This is impure, I am pure.

- He is ignorant, I am knowledgeable.

- He is of small caste; I am of big caste.

- His religion is small, my religion is big.

- This is the cover, I am golden. I am

- This is a monster; I am a god.

- He is a slave, I am free.

- He is my servant; I am his God.

- He has no rights; I have all the rights. This is so -

Such a person thinks when he is trapped in the quagmire of knowledge.

Dear friend, what does a wise man think about others? Is such as -

- Whether black or white, all are equal human beings.

- No human being is impure by birth, a liar or a dishonest person.

- is impure, everything else is sacred.

- Despite being knowledgeable, consider yourself ignorant.

- There is no small caste or big caste, everyone is a slave.

- No religion is big or small. Religion is the name of truth and honesty.

- We all have the same flesh and blood; we are all human beings.

- There is no demon or God, a human being is a human being.

- Everyone has the right to be free.

- No human being is anyone's servant and no human being is anyone's God. Everyone can live as a master.

- A knowledgeable person would think that people all over the world should have equal rights.

Dear friend, I have placed before you 10 examples of a human being trapped in the slavery of high and low i.e. ignorance and I have also placed before you 10 examples of a knowledgeable person i.e. one who is out of the slavery of high and low. If you have any idea about what is slavery of high and low in these 20 examples. If you are not able to understand the matter, then you should study the true knowledge of great men, only then you will be able to understand this thing. And dear friend, you are saying that high and low is a part of Hindu religion. Dear two, can high and low not be a part of Hindu religion because religion is the name of truth and honesty which is not high and low and discrimination. Eliminates. If there is high and low in any religion, then it cannot be a religion, it can be a conspiracy of slavery to mislead in the name of religion, nothing else.

Question-25. Friend, what is inferiority complex? Why have you called inferiority complex as slavery and if inferiority complex is slavery, then how can a person come out of it?

Answer - Dear friend, inferiority complex is the feeling which weakens a person from within and stops him from doing good work. Many types of thoughts arise in his mind. Such as -

- I am a despicable person.

- I am not worthy of this work.

- I can't do this work.

- I am to serve others.

- I am not able to read and write.

- What kind of judge will I become after studying?

- No one in our family can do any good work.

- What great work will we do to get a reward?

- Whatever work our elders have been doing, we will also do the same work.

- We are the poorest and weakest human beings in this world.

Dear friend, all this is the result of inferiority complex, we can call it slavery of inferiority complex and inferiority complex. If you want to get out of inferiority complex, then you have to keep the following things in mind. Such as -

1. You belong to a small caste.
2. You are untouchable.
3. You can't do anything.
4. You are born only to serve.
5. By which education will you become CM, PM, MP.
6. Nothing is in your control. Is
7. You will do the work of your fathers and grandfathers.
8. You can never move forward.
9. You can never become a scholar.
10. We belong to high caste etc.

All these things will have to be abandoned. Whoever gives up all these things and embraces truth and honesty from his heart will be saved forever from the slavery of inferiority complex and will also become successful.

Question-26. Friends, those who consider themselves special (capable) are also slaves. Can you please explain this clearly?

Answer - Dear friend, considering yourself special means considering yourself different and considering others different such as -

- I am the best person on this earth.

- I have come to rule the world.

- All other humans in front of me are animals.

- I remain free and everyone else remains my slave.

- May I get every happiness in the world and may everyone else remain unhappy.

- I will become the richest person in the world and everyone else will remain poor.

- People called me great but everyone else remained fool.

- People of the world may greet me and I may not even respond to them.

- There should be only my name in the entire world.

- May only I rule the whole world etc.

Dear friend, these 10 examples that we have given are all signs of mental slavery, this is called slavery of being special. If man wants to be free from this slavery, then he should consider the people of the whole world as equal and he should help the world for the welfare of all, only then he can come out of this slavery.

Question-27. Friend, how can we recognize the slavery of the mind and how can a person get out of the slavery of the mind?

Answer - Dear friend, very few people know about the slavery of the mind and most of the people do not even know what the mind is. Very few people know about how we can identify the mind and whether the mind is free or slave. Dear friend, it is only after serious thinking about the slavery of the mind that one realizes what kind of slavery the mind is like, as when a person is a slave, he also has some master. It is the same way when the mind is a slave then its master is a lie. It happens. Just as a master makes his slave do a lot of work for free, in the same way a lie makes the mind do very big wrong things.

Come let's know what lies do to the enslaved mind -

Lies make the mind dishonest.

- Lies manipulate the mind.
- Lies betray the heart.
- Lies cause murder from the mind.
- Lies deceive the mind.
- Lies steal from the mind.
- Lies corrupt the mind.
- Lies rape the mind.
- Lies make the mind discriminate against others.

- Lies make the heart hate other religions.

- Lies make the mind call lies again and again.

- A lie makes the mind prove a lie to be true.

- A lie makes other people call impure from the heart.

- Lies make others call themselves untouchable.

- People with false hearts in the name of God

- gets robbed.

- A false mind misleads people in the name of heaven and hell

Right

- Lies make the mind speak about heaven and hell.

- The false mind makes one worship graves and stones.

- Lies create disunity in the mind.

- Lies create misbehavior in the mind.

- Lies make the mind ignorant and foolish.

- Lie is a devil in the mind and turns it into a devil.

- Lies create fear in the mind.

- Lies create sorrow and worries in the mind.

- God, God, Allah, Wahe Guru make the false mind

- The one God who has many names breaks it apart.

Lies trouble its slave minds a lot. Troubled mind troubles the body. All the sorrows of the body are born due to becoming a slave. A mind trapped in slavery neither lets a person sleep peacefully nor wake up peacefully. People are trapped in slavery all the time. Keeps troubling the mind. The mind has become a slave because of lies. Lies are the root of all problems. How can we free the slave mind?

If the slave mind truly accepts the truth, then it will be freed from the slavery of lies. When the truth settles in the mind, I will try to tell you through a poem what the truth will give to the mind.

If the truth is in the mind, then the mind will improve.

If there is a lie in the mind, then the mind will get spoiled.

If there is truth in the mind, then life will progress.

If there are lies in the mind, then life will be destroyed.

If there is truth in the mind, then a person will be happy.

If it is true, then man will love everyone.

If there is truth in the mind, then the truth will eliminate hatred from within.

If there is truth in the mind, then it will fill the person with love from within.

If the truth is in the mind, then the truth will make a person a scholar.

If truth is in the mind, then truth will make a person great.

If there is truth in the mind, then a person will not believe in caste.

If the truth is true, then a person will not believe in the caste system.

If there is truth in the mind, then a person will not consider anyone high or low.

If there is truth in the mind, then a person will not believe in casteism and racism.

If there is truth in the mind, then a person will not consider anyone untouchable.

If there is truth in the mind, then a person will not discriminate against anyone.

If there is truth in the mind, then he will not hate people of other religions.

If there is truth in the mind, then a person will love people of all religions.

If there is truth in the mind, then a person will become wise.

If there is truth in the mind, then a person will become powerful.

If there is truth in the mind, then a person will embrace the poor and the oppressed.

If there is truth in the mind, then a person will love the poor and the oppressed.

If there is truth in the mind, then a person will help the poor.

If there is truth in the mind, then a person will be kind to everyone.

If there is truth in the mind then a person will become compassionate.

If there is truth in the mind then a person will become a characterful person.

If there is truth in the mind then a person will not be happy to hear his praise.

If there is truth in the mind then a person will not feel sad after hearing his evil.

If there is truth in the mind then a person will not be afraid of any devil.

If there is truth in the mind then a person will not bow down to any devil.

If there is truth in the mind then a person will not scare anyone.

If there is truth in the mind then a person will not be afraid of anyone.

If truth is in the mind, then a person will never worship.

If there is truth in the mind then a person will not be afraid to even of the fear of death.

If there is truth in the mind then a person will not be afraid of the things like heaven and hell.

If the truth is in the mind, then a person will not believe in the talk of hell and heaven.

If there is truth in the mind then a person will be saved from lust, anger, greed, attachment, ego and greed.

If there is truth in the mind then a person will become patient, content, tolerant and equal.

If there is truth in the mind, then a person will spread the truth throughout the world.

If truth is there in the mind, then the whole world will become a family for a person.

Meghraj Singh Only a true person will be able to meet his God Allah Waheguru God while alive.

Question-28. Friend, you have told about the slavery of mind. If a person's mind gets spoiled, then also talk about what harm is caused by the spoiled mind.

Answer - Dear friend, when the mind gets disturbed, then the disturbed mind causes a lot of harm to the person. I will try to tell you what harm a disturbed mind does through a poem such as -

If there is a lie in the mind, then the mind will get spoiled.

If the truth is in the mind, then the mind will improve.

If there is a lie in the mind, then a person will continue to believe in the caste and caste system.

If there is a lie in the mind, then a person will continue to believe in untouchability and high and low.

If there is a lie in the mind, then the person will be proud of the high caste and will become proud of the low caste.

Will remain trapped in inferiority complex.

If there is a lie in the mind, then a person will continue to discriminate and hate other people.

If there are lies in the mind, then a person will keep hating people of other religions.

If there is a lie in the mind, then a person will keep calling his own religion big and other's religion small.

If there is a lie in the mind, then a person will become dishonest.

If there is a lie in the mind, then a person will become a devil.

If there is a lie in the mind, then a person will not become a devil.

If there is a lie in the mind, then a person will become greedy.

If there is a lie in the mind then a person will become a rapist.

If there is a lie in the mind then a person will become evil.

If there is a lie in the mind then a person will become a conspirator.

If there is a lie in the mind then a person will become corrupt.

If there is a lie in the mind then a person will become a thief and a robber.

If there is a lie in the mind then a person will become a treacherous fraudster.

If there is a lie in the mind then a person will rob people and eat them in the name of heaven and hell.

If there is a lie in the mind then a person will rob and eat people in the name of hell and heaven.

If there is a lie in the mind then a person will make others worship stones.

If there is a lie in the mind then a person will make others worship the graves.

If there is a lie in the mind, then a person will become a murderer.

If there is a lie in the mind, then the person will become ignorant.

If there is a lie in the mind, then a person will become a cheater.

If there is a lie in the mind, then a person will become clever.

If there is a lie in the mind, then a person will become an enemy of his own people also.

If there is a lie in the mind then a person will never be able to make his loved ones his own.

If there is a lie in the mind, then a person will become a cheater.

If there is a lie in the mind then a person will become clever.

If there is a lie in the mind, then a person will consider himself smart.

If there is a lie in the mind, then a person will consider others as fools.

If there is a lie in the mind then mental suffering will arise inside.

If there is a lie in the mind then all the happiness of a person will end.

If there is a lie in the mind then a person will ruin his own life.

If there is a lie in the mind then a person will destroy the life of his family also.

If there is a lie in the mind then a person will not be able to understand even the knowledge of religious scriptures.

If there is a lie in the mind then a person will never be able to become a scholar and a great person.

If there is a lie in the mind then a person can have all the wealth in the world.

Still, he will remain a beggar.

If there is a lie in the mind then a person will remain a murderer and hunter of innocent people.

Even liars will accept the truth wholeheartedly.

Because of the truth he will be saved from mental suffering forever.

Truth will generate supreme knowledge within them and then one day they will become great.

Meghraj Singh: Only true human beings will be freed from the fear of death by the grace of Guru.

Question-29. Friend, you will be speaking very wise and thoughtful things. Okay, let's ask one more question, why is hatred spreading in the whole world? I see how knowledgeable you are considering yourself to be, let us also see whether your knowledge is right or wrong?

Answer - Dear friend, there are many problems in the whole world due to which hatred is spreading in the whole world, but two problems are main.

1. Casteism
2. Racism

Because of these two problems, a lot of hatred is spreading throughout the world. Because of these two problems, people are fighting among themselves and countries are fighting with each other. I will try to tell you about the reasons behind these two problems, how hatred is arising and how these problems can be eliminated, such as -

Is casteism and racism within the world very terrible and dangerous for humans?

Casteism and racism create hatred inside a human being, due to which a person feels hatred and jealousy towards another human being, due to which the good qualities in a human being die, due to which a human being keeps walking on the fire of hatred inside again and again, hence, humans all over the world. For casteism and racism are very terrible and dangerous.

How can we remove casteism and racism?

We can end casteism and racism as if all the great men who have been born in the whole world like Gautam Buddha, Jesus, Muhammad Saheb, Saint Ravidas, Saint Namdev, Saint Kabir Das, Saint Farid, Guru Nanak Saheb, Guru Govind Singh etc. will adopt the path of truth. He will be saved from casteism and racism forever.

Note - Any person who adopts truth and honesty wholeheartedly will be saved from casteism and racism forever.

Dear friend, whatever you have said that makes me consider myself knowledgeable, I am considering myself knowledgeable. Dear friend, I want to tell you one special thing, what I am writing is not of my own free will, I am just God, God, Waheguhe Ru, Allah who is the only one. There are many names of the God who is a huge power.

I am writing as per his wish. There are no millions, but billions of creatures like me on this earth to whom God is providing food and water and everything. I am a small human being on this earth, and I am nothing else.

Question-30. Second, if we look carefully at the whole world, there are many religions in the whole world, there are many religious places and the people propagating the religion would be not only millions but crores. Friends, explain why despite so many religions, so many religious places and so many preachers, they could not eliminate hatred from within the entire world, what are the reasons behind this?

Answer - Dear friend, all the questions you have asked till now were easy for me, but this question you have asked is the most dangerous and crooked. Friend, very few people ask such questions and very few people have the answers to such questions.

Dear friend, since you have asked this question, I am fully prepared to answer it.

I will try. Friends, hatred has not ended all over the world because religious people have not understood the knowledge of religion. My personal experience says that -

If we follow religion without thinking then it will take the form of slavery.

If we follow religion thoughtfully, it will take the form of freedom.

I am trying to tell you about this issue through a poem such as -

- The knowledge of religion is very distorted and not every human being can understand it.

No one wants to understand the words of one who has understood the knowledge of religion.

- Those who fight on the issue of religion cannot be religious people.

Only those who think about religion can be religious people

- If we are hating anyone after seeing their religion then we are not a religious person. If we are rising above caste and religion and loving everyone equally then we are a religious person.

- If there are lies and dishonesty within us, then we are not a religious person at all.

- If we have truth and honesty then we can consider ourselves a religious person.

- If we consider ourselves very smart then we will not understand religion.

- If we consider ourselves a student then we will understand the point of religion.

- If we consider ourselves to be from a high caste or a high clan, then we will not understand the matter of religion at all.

- If we consider ourselves a human being rising above caste and religion, then we will understand the point of religion.

- If we are killing animals in the name of any kind of religion then we are not religious people, we are just common humans.

- If we are realizing our Lord within all living beings, then we can be religious human beings.

- If we are misleading people and telling lies by wearing the clothes of religion then we are not religious people.

- If we are speaking the truth and showing people the path of truth even without wearing the clothes of religion, then we are religious people.

- If any person does not believe in any religion, if we are calling him irreligious or infidel, then we are not a religious person.

- If we are explaining any religious thing to any person, then understand that we are religious people.

- If any person is creating riots and spreading hatred in the name of religion, then he is not a religious person at all.

- If any person is spreading love in the world in the name of religion and showing the path of truth, then he is a religious person.

- If we are lying, being dishonest, stealing, robbing or cheating then it is not God's order.

- If we are telling the truth, working honestly and winning people's trust, then this is God's order.

- If we are staying hungry, taking bath in any pilgrimage or practicing hypocrisy, it is not the order of God.

- If we are eating our own hard work, feeding others too, not taking any kind of pilgrimage, not making unnecessary donations, then this is God's order.

- If we are praying to our Lord in the morning and evening and are lying the whole day, then our Lord will not be happy with this.

- If we are not even praying morning and evening and are speaking the truth every moment and chanting God's name internally, then our God will be happy.

- If we are causing any kind of pain to our body in the name of religion, God will not be happy with it.

- If we are serving people with our bodies in the name of religion and spreading love in the world, God will be happy with this.

- If we are causing any kind of pain to our body in the name of religion, God will not be happy with it.

- If we are serving people with our bodies in the name of religion and spreading love in the world, God will be happy with this.

- If we are torturing Muslims and the poor in the name of religion, then God will not be happy with it.

- If we are helping the poor and the oppressed in the name of religion and are serving our parents then God will be happy.

- Listen to the truth, speak the truth, settle the truth in the mind, this is the real religion.

- Work hard yourself, teach others to work hard, speak the truth yourself, teach others to speak the truth, this is the duty of religion.

- Whether we will get heaven or hell after death, all these are imaginary things, stay away from these things.

- Accept this that you will get the same results in your lifetime as per your actions.

- Those people who shed the blood of others in the name of religion, they will be blessed with nymphs in heaven after their death.

- You will find that this is wrong.

- It is true that those people who do good deeds in the name of religion and embrace the joys will attain supreme peace while alive.

- Those people who do bad deeds will keep burning in the fire of hell and hell for their entire life. They will get the fruits of their bad deeds while they are alive.

- Those people who do good deeds will live their entire life in heaven and heaven. They will get the fruits of their good deeds during their lifetime.

- God Allah Ha Bhagwan Wahe Guhe Ru. Those who consider these separately will never understand the matter of religion, nor will any experienced knowledge develop in them. God Allah Bhagwan Waheguhe Ru, only those who understand these names as the names of only one God will understand the matter of religion and one day experienced knowledge will grow within them.

- Only people with experienced knowledge will see not only their own family but the entire world as their own family.

- By the grace of Guru Meghraj Singh, only true people will find ultimate happiness and true God from within.

Hatred has spread throughout the world because religious people have not spread the knowledge of religion properly throughout the world. That is why today bad people are burning in the fire of hatred and if they adopt truth and honesty then they will come out of the fire of hatred and will be able to live with love.

Question-31. Friend, you get scared after seeing the question, no question is dangerous, you have already answered this question. Hey friend, my next question is that among women and men all over the world, who is more mentally stronger, a woman or a man? Please clarify about this?

Answer - Dear friend, what food have you eaten today due to which you are asking the most dangerous questions today? If I say men are more powerful than women will go after me and if I say women are more powerful than men will go after me. Dear friend, now I have to answer your question. Whether men are following me or women are following me, I will definitely answer your question. According to my personal experience, women are mentally stronger all over the world.

Dear friend, you must be thinking that if men are ruling the entire world, then how can women be mentally stronger. Friends, you are not alone in thinking like this, almost 90% of the people think so and also consider it to be true that in the whole world only men are mentally stronger than women. Friends, I have called women mentally stronger than men because I have experienced this. Dear friend, let me tell you a special thing, almost 99% of the women in the whole world do not even know that they are mentally stronger than men because I have experienced this.

- We don't call those women mentally strong who beat men with sticks and brooms.

- Psychologically, we call those women powerful who teach men to live with truth and faith.

Women are mentally stronger than men in such ways as -

- The mental condition of women is much more powerful than the mental condition of men.

- The mental state of 90% of the women all over the world is such that no matter whether it is wrong or right, women never back down from their point.

- If a woman's mental state is in this state of incomprehension, then not even 10 men or 100 men together can make her understand.

- If a woman's mental state is in a state of understanding then can she explain it to 10 men or to 100 men?

- If women adopt truth and honesty wholeheartedly, they themselves will move from the state of ignorance to the state of understanding.

- Then after that there will be only happiness in the life of the entire family, and then she will lead her entire family to a state of understanding.

- A foolish woman will fight over small matters, speak loudly, insult everyone and, considering herself smart, will make everyone's situation worse. A wise woman will resolve big conflicts through talks and with great tolerance.

- Will never speak loudly, will respect everyone, and will consider herself a common woman. She will understand and keep her family happy all the time.

- If intelligent women from all over the world will propagate truth and honesty, then the whole world will become prosperous.

- Only wise women all over the world can take very good care of the health, food and drink of the people all over the world and of their families.

If women follow the path of truth and honesty then only, they will be able to recognize that they are mentally stronger than men.

Question-32. Friend, after listening to you, it seems that you have a lot of knowledge about religion. A question arises again and again in my mind that the amount of blood that is being shed in the world due to religious fanaticism is not equal to the amount of blood that has been shed in the world's wars and conflicts, and this question is not only in my mind but in the minds of millions of people. And I think this question is very difficult for you but I want the answer to this question 100%?

Answer - Dear friend, when did you start thinking that I have any knowledge of religion? I am just a student who tries to learn something from people. Dear friend, this question is arising in your mind, earlier this question was also arising in my mind and even now this question is arising in my mind, but you are the leader, you have asked the answer to this question from me and this question is also in the mind of crores of people. That is why I will try to answer this question completely.

Dear friend, you raised the question that due to religious fanaticism, the amount of blood that is being shed in the world is not equal to that in wars and conflicts. Friend, you are not alone in asking this question. Almost 90% of the people in the world believe this to be true and this is true. We also believe in this, but my personal belief is that the thinking of crores of people may be right according to them, but I think about it in this way that first we will talk about religious fanaticism, then we will talk about whether blood has been shed because of religious fanaticism or non-religious fanaticism. We will talk about the reason blood has been shed. **Dear friend, there are two types of religious fanaticism such as -**

1. Religious fundamentalism
2. Irreligious fundamentalism

Religious fundamentalism - Friend, according to my personal experience, we call it as -

- Tell the truth.

- Raising voice against oppression.

- To teach a lesson to the oppressors.

- To embrace the oppressed and the poor.

- To give a befitting reply to liars.

- To eliminate hatred from within people.

- Spreading the truth throughout the world.

- Treating people all over the world as equal.

- Consider people from all over the world as your family.

- Bhagwan, God, Allah, Waheguhe Ru, there are many names of one power for everyone, that is to pray for the welfare of everyone ahead on the path, etc.

Dear friends, all these are examples of religious fanaticism. This religious fanaticism brings only happiness in human life.

Dear friend, all these are examples of irreligious fanaticism. This fanaticism brings only sorrow in people's lives.

Dear friend, people believe that due to religious fanaticism, a lot of blood has been shed in the world, but I believe that it is not because of religious fanaticism but because of irreligious fanaticism that blood has been shed throughout the world because -

If religious people fight a war, it will be for the freedom of humanity.

If irreligious people fight a war, it will be to enslave humanity.

The war of religious people will be for the benefit of all.

The war of irreligious people will be only for their own benefit.

Those who fight for the poor and the oppressed will be called religious fundamentalists.

Those who shed the blood of the poor and the oppressed will be called irreligious fundamentalists.

Those who spread love and knowledge in the name of religion are called religious fanatics.

Those who create riots and spread hatred in the name of religion are called religious fanatics.

If even the irreligious adopt truth and honesty, they will improve.

Meghraj Singh: Only because of religious people, people all over the world will be able to live peacefully.

Dear friend, I personally believe that the people who shed blood in the name of religion were not actually religious people, they killed humanity by wearing the clothes of religion. One who kills humanity cannot be a religious person. Their fight was not a religious fight. Their fight was only a fight to fulfill their kingdom, land, property or their pride or we can also call it a fight to fulfill their personal interest, it is not a fight of religion at all.

Can it be said or cannot be linked to the name of religion. We can call a religious fight a fight which The battle was fought to provide rights to the poor or to protect them or to end oppression. Dear friend, very few wars have been fought in the whole world which have been fought to protect humanity or to end oppression. Most of the wars have been fought to fulfill one's selfishness, which have been fought in the name of religion, that is why today almost 90% of the people think that the amount of blood that humanity has shed due to religious fanaticism is not equal to the amount of blood that humanity has shed in other wars.

Dear friend, I am saying this clearly and with full confidence that blood is not being shed in the whole world because of religious fanaticism but because of irreligious fanaticism. Only true and honest people can understand this. Only true and honest people are religious. We are human beings and I feel that you too must have understood this because you also consider yourself a religious person, that is why you are asking me religious questions.

Question-33. Friend, when did I say that I am a religious person, I am just trying to ask you a question on the issue of religion. Come on, leave aside the issue of whether I am religious or irreligious, you answer me the next question as you have said in the answer to the previous question that I am a person of religious fanaticism. It is not because of this that blood has been shed, but because of irreligious fanaticism, blood has been shed all over the world. Now tell me who spread this irreligious fanaticism in the entire world, and who are the people behind it?

Answer: Dear friend, you are asking very terrible questions. You are testing me by asking such questions. Whether you test me or not, I will still answer your question. Dear friend, irreligious fanaticism has spread all over the world because of Brahmins and Jews because they consider themselves to be the most religious people in the world and what they consider as religious fanaticism, according to me or according to my personal experience, is irreligious fanaticism because of which they have no knowledge about religion and irreligion. What Brahmins and Jews are considering as religion, we can also call it mental slavery, that is, Brahmins and Jews are trapped in the fanaticism of mental slavery and both of them have also trapped the people of the whole world in the fanaticism of mental slavery.

Brahmins and Jews are guilty of irreligious fanaticism and Brahmins and Jews are the biggest mentally enslaved people in the world. Dear friend, even Brahmins and Jews do not know that they are trapped in mental slavery. The day Brahmins and Jews accept the truth, they will come out of mental slavery.

Question-34. Friend, you talk very big but you do not have even a single penny of experience and knowledge. You have given the answer to my question absolutely nonsense. Well, how can Brahmins and Jews be mental slaves? Brahmins and Jews are ruling the entire world. How can those who rule be mental slaves?

Answer - Dear friend, I have called Brahmins and Jews mental slaves because they do not want to see others free and those people who are slaves themselves cannot see others free, **such as -**

Brahmins and Jews believe that they are the most knowledgeable people on this earth, they are gods and they are the most powerful people. In reality, they believe this for themselves and consider others as animals and insects and also oppress others and enslave others. Even though they try to do good, they try to enslave others only those who are trapped in mental slavery, that is why both Brahmins and Jews are very mentally. There are people trapped in slavery.

- Brahmins and Jews waste their precious power in enslaving others.

- In order to enslave others, they put themselves and their entire families at stake.

- Those who boast that they have no power are mental slaves from within.

- Ignorant people are the ones who do not have the intelligence to salute themselves.

- The ideology of Brahmins and Jews makes them mental slaves and traps both of them in mental slavery.

- Due to casteism, varna system and racism, both these ideologies ruin their lives.

- If Brahmins and Jews abandon their ideology, they will become free from mental slavery.

- You yourself will be happy, others will also be happy, and the lives of Brahmins and Jews will never be ruined again.

- The person who is free from mental slavery will never trap anyone in mental slavery.

- He himself will live a life of freedom and will teach others to live a life of freedom as well.

Question-35. Friends, how should women all over the world use their mental strength properly?

Answer - Dear friend, if women all over the world take special care of these things, then they will be able to use their mental strength properly, such as - If women lie, be dishonest, gossip, fight over things, think bad about others. , will consider themselves very smart, will consider their family members and others stupid etc. then women are misusing their mental power due to which their body will suffer a lot.

If women tell the truth, work honestly and resolve domestic disputes through dialogue, will not consider anyone a fool, will not consider themselves smart, will not get angry at anyone, and will look after their families with great love, then women will fully utilize their mental strength. It is being used which will be very beneficial for women's body.

Note – Those women who truly embrace truth and honesty will be able to use their mental power properly and this will benefit their body immensely due to which they will be happy themselves and will be able to give happiness to their family too.

Question-36. Friends, how should men all over the world use their mental strength properly?

Answer - Dear friend, if men all over the world take special care of these things, then they will be able to use their mental strength properly, such as - if men lie, commit dishonesty, commit corruption, commit atrocities, consider women as slaves, look down on others and elevate themselves. If they consider others as ignorant and themselves as wise, then men are misusing their mental power which will cause great harm to their body due to which they will remain troubled throughout their life.

If men speak the truth, work honestly, treat women as equals, neither oppress anyone nor do corruption, will not consider anyone else low and themselves high, will not consider themselves knowledgeable and others ignorant, will love everyone equally. Men are using their mental strength properly which will greatly benefit their body due to which they will remain happy throughout their life.

Note – Any man who truly embraces truth and honesty will be able to use his mental power properly, due to which he will be able to live a happy life throughout his life.

Question-37. Friend, all religious people do religious work so that their mind becomes peaceful and many religious people also say that I am doing religious work for peace of mind, or I am doing religious work for peace of mind. Friend, the mind of those who do religious work is How to identify whether the person has calmed down or not?

Answer - Dear friend, people of different religions all over the world do religious work so that their mind becomes calm. How will people of different religions identify **whether their mind is peaceful or disturbed, such as -**

- If he is doing this despite doing religious work. Are such as -

- If he is lying or dishonest, then his mind is not at peace.

- If he is greedy, mischievous, corrupt, then his mind is not at peace.

- If there is casteism and racism within them, then their mind is not at peace.

- If he has hatred or discrimination against others, then his mind is not at peace.

- If he is feeling jealous after seeing the rich and hates seeing the poor, then his mind is not calmed down.

- If he is afraid of seeing the rich and imposing his authority on the poor, then his mind is not at peace.

- If he is deceiving or blackmailing, then his mind is not at peace.

- If he is cheating or betraying, then his mind is not at peace.

- If he is robbing others in the name of God, in the name of Allah, in the name of God, then his mind is not at peace.

- If they are looting people by luring them with the lure of heaven and hell and threatening them with hell, then their minds are not at peace.

- If they are fighting over small things at home and hitting each other, then their mind is not at peace.

- If he is gossiping about others and instigating fights in other people's homes, then his mind is not at peace.

- If he considers himself superior and others inferior, then his mind is not at peace.

- If he is considering himself inferior and others are superior, then his mind is not at peace.

- If he is playing tricks on others, or is fooling others, then his mind is not at peace.

- If he is demanding more by offering a little money at religious places, then his mind is not at peace.

- If his conscience is still dead even after doing religious work, then his mind has not become calm.

- If he is harassing the poor and the downtrodden and taking away their rights, then his mind is not at peace.

- If the mind remains disturbed, the inside will be filled with demerits and all religious activities will fail.

- If the mind is calm, only good qualities develop within and all religious activities become successful.

- Once you get the truth, your mind becomes calm, all the demerits are erased from within and then there is light of knowledge within.

- People of different religions all over the world, black, white, brown, should all be seen as members of our family.

Note - Whoever the people of the whole world will accept the truth and honesty in their heart, their mind will become calm, then they will see the whole world as their own and then they will live life in ultimate happiness.

Question-38. Friend, if the mind has become calm after doing religious work or any good work, then how should we identify it?

Answer - Dear friend, after doing religious work, the mind becomes calm. We can identify the calm mind like -

if he is doing this after doing religious work. Are such as -

- If he is telling the truth and is working honestly then his mind is at peace.

- If he is not lying and is not dishonest then his mind is at peace.

- If there is no greed, greed or attachment in them then their mind is calm.

- If he is not tricking and conspiring then his mind is at peace.

- If he is solving big disputes through talks then his mind is at peace.

- If he is not speaking ill of anyone and is explaining everything to everyone lovingly, then his mind is at peace.

- If he is respecting others and is getting himself respected, then his mind is at peace.

- If he does not consider himself very smart and others are stupid, then his mind is at peace.

- If there is no inferiority complex and pride in them then their mind is calm.

- If there is no casteism and discrimination within them then their mind is at peace.

- If he is not considering himself the best and others are inferior, then his mind is at peace.

- If he is not considering himself inferior and others as superior, then his mind is at peace.

- If he himself is eating after working hard and is also feeding others, then his mind is at peace.

- If he is respecting the rich and the poor equally, then his mind is at peace.

- If he is not jealous on seeing the rich and not hating on seeing the poor, then his mind is at peace.

- If he is not afraid of the rich and is not imposing authority over the rich, then his mind is at peace

- If he is not robbing people in the name of Allah, God, God, Waheguhe Ru then his mind is at peace.

- If they are not looting people by showing greed for heaven and heaven and fear of hell and hell then their mind is at peace.

- If he is seeing one God within the people of the whole world, then his mind is at peace.

- If he is praying to one God daily for the welfare of the people of the whole world, then the mind is calm.

- If the mind finds the truth, then there will be light of knowledge within the mind.

- With the light of true knowledge, ignorance will be erased from the mind.

- If the mind is calm, then the mind is in the form of God. Only the mind with the form of God will see the whole world as its own.

- If the mind is disturbed, then it is the form of the devil. The whole world will appear different to the mind having the form of the devil.

- If he is showing the path of truth to the people of the whole world by considering him as his family, then his mind is at peace.

- If he considers the whole world as his family and loves people all over the world equally, then his mind is at peace.

- Note - All the people in the whole world who will truly adopt truth and honesty from their heart, their mind will become calm, then the religious work done by them will also be successful, and they will also get supreme happiness. If you find a true Guru, your mind will become calm and happiness will arise in a calm mind. By the grace of Meghraj Singh Sachguru, all the works of religion become successful.

Question-39. Friend, sometimes our mind gives us a lot of happiness, and sometimes it gives us a lot of sorrow. What is the reason behind this? Tell us clearly why the mind does this?

Answer - Dear friend, the mind is the owner of many amazing dual powers inside the human being. If the mind adopts the truth, then it becomes the form of God and gives happiness to the human being, and if the mind adopts the lie, then the mind becomes the form of the devil and gives only sorrow to the human being. **Is such as -**

The mind is the form of God, the mind is the form of the devil.

The mind itself is the form of the being, the mind itself is the form of the human being. ,

If there is truth in the mind then man is the form of God.

If there is a lie in the mind then a person is a form of devil.

If there is greed in the mind, then the person is a devil.

If there is no deceit or fraud in the mind then a person is a human being.

If there is truth in the mind then a person will do good work for 12 months.

If there is a lie in the mind then a person will do bad things for 12 months.

If there is greed in the mind then a person will rob people for 12 months.

If there is no deceit in the mind then a person will do normal work.,

If there is truth in the mind then a person will talk about knowledge and science.

If there is a lie in the mind, then a person will talk about worshiping stones and graves.

If there is greed in the mind then a person will talk about killing others.

If there is no deceit or fraud in the mind then a person will only talk about his livelihood.

If there is truth in the mind then a person will show the path of truth to others.

If there is a lie in the mind then a person will mislead others.

If there is greed in the mind then a person will make others greedy also.

If there is no deceit or deceit in the mind then a person will make others ordinary also.

If there is truth in the mind then a person will talk about knowledge and science.

If there is a lie in the mind then a person will talk about worshiping stones and graves.

If there is greed in the mind, then a person will talk about killing others.

If there is no deceit or deceit in the mind, then a person will only talk about his livelihood. ——

If there is truth in the mind, then a person will show the path of truth to others.

If there is a lie in the mind, then a person will mislead others.

If there is greed in the mind, then a person will make others greedy also.

If there is no deceit or deceit in the mind, then a person will make others ordinary also.,

If man is the form of God, then he will embrace people with love.

If man is the form of devil, then he will scare others in the name of heaven, hell, hell and heaven.

If a human being is a devil, then he will teach others to do corruption and rape.

If a person is an ordinary person, then he will teach others to live with love.,

If a person is truthful then he will neither fear any army nor will he scare anyone.

If a person is a liar, then he himself will get scared and will scare others too.

If a person is greedy, he will trap himself and trap others too.

If a person is not deceitful then he himself will be happy and will teach others to live happily. ——

With the true knowledge of great men, the devil is evil and everyone who is greedy will become good people.

Even ordinary people will become great scholars with the true knowledge of great men.

Only those who spread the truth will be called the embodiment of God in this world.

Meghraj Singh Only true people will be remembered in the world for many centuries. ——-

Question-40. Friends, tell me some easy way for children to improve their mind, youth to improve their mind, women to improve their mind and elderly and all other people to improve their mind?

Answer - Dear friend, the mind is like an earth. Just like the seed a person sows inside the earth, a person gets the same fruit. Similarly, if a person sows a seed of lie in his mind, he will get its result. If he sows a seed of truth in his mind, he will also get its result. Like for example -

We plant trees and seek the fruits of sorrow and happiness.

The mind is like the earth, it reaps the fruits as it sows.

If you sow lies in your mind, you will reap the fruits of sorrow; if you sow truth in your mind, you will reap the fruits of happiness.

Lies are the seeds of sorrow. If there is a lie in the mind then where will happiness come from.

Hatred, ego, pride and inequality will arise inside and worries will haunt you throughout your life.

Truth is the seed of happiness. If there is truth in the mind then there will be no sorrow.

Love, humility and equality will develop inside and then the whole life will be filled with happiness.

The condition of man is such that he works for the sake of suffering and asks for happiness from his Lord.

When people suffer in return for their work, they curse their Lord.

What are the painful actions that cause sorrow such as -

1. Lying and being dishonest create mental suffering in the mind.

2. Corruption, misconduct, atrocities cause mental suffering.

3. Theft, robbery and looting in the name of God cause mental suffering.

4. Cheating, hatred, discrimination cause mental suffering.

5. Mental suffering also arises in those who fear hell and hell and those who covet heaven and paradise.

If a person does even one of the above-mentioned tasks, then even millions of doctors in the world cannot cure him because -

One whose mind is unhappy, his body is unhappy, only if the unhappy mind truly accepts the truth. Gradually, mental suffering will truly end from within him.

What are those works which create happiness due to which a person always becomes **happy, such as -**

1. Speaking the truth and working honestly create mental happiness.

2. Good conduct, good behavior and thinking generate mental happiness.

3. Preventing others from doing bad things and showing them the right path creates mental happiness.

4. Becoming worthy of trust, having good character and keeping intentions clean generate mental happiness. Mental happiness is also generated in those who avoid the imaginary names of hell, heaven and hell, and those who show the path of truth to people and spread the truth in the world.

Note - All the people in the whole world who will keep the truth in their mind, all their wishes will be fulfilled, and then they will live happily throughout their life.

Some important, amazing poetry

If the mind truly accepts the truth, then man will become the form of God.

If the mind really accepts lies then the human being will become a form of devil.

Man runs outside to do bad deeds, that is why he keeps wandering.

A person who does good work gets connected within and hence remains happy.

Those who do bad things definitely get punishment, it is the result of their actions.

Those who do good work get respect, it is the result of their deeds.

Those who do good deeds, whether they live for one year or a hundred years, they become history.

Whether those who do evil deeds live for one year or a hundred years, their names are buried.

Good people will also die, bad people will also die, everyone has to die one day.

Bad people die the death of conscience every day, but good people die only once.

Bad people remain trapped in the fear of hell and the greed for heaven and heaven.

They commit bad deeds throughout their life and finally die in agony.

Good people rise above the greed of hell, heaven and heaven.

Meghraj Singh A true human being finds his Lord within himself by the grace of Guru.

Note - Why man came to this earth and why he is leaving, only God knows or the true Guru knows, but why have we all come and what have we come to do, we have almost written about it by the grace of the Guru, this is the true truth. Only a human being can recognize, may the Guru please show everyone the path of truth and make them meet their Lord from within themselves.

Mysterious and amazing information related to the life of humans all over the world.

Question-41. Friends, which is the right way to live life and how many different ways are people living their lives across the world?

Answer - Dear friend, according to my personal experience, people all over the world are living life following **3 types of paths such as -**

People all over the world adopt three methods such as -

1. The first path of life is to lie.

2. Another way of life – sometimes lying, sometimes telling the truth.

3. The third way of life – telling the truth.

First way of life - Those people who tell only lies in life, dishonesty comes in them, corruption comes in them due to which many problems come in their life, they get only sorrows in their whole life.

Second way of life - People who sometimes lie and sometimes tell the truth, such people sometimes become honest, and sometimes they become dishonest, the progress of such people's life stops, they get sorrow no matter what they say, they get happiness anywhere.

Third way of life - Honesty is born in the people who speak the truth, equality, humanity and humanity are born in them and such people get only happiness throughout their life.

Note - People all over the world should truly adopt truth and honesty in their lives and find ultimate happiness from within themselves.

Question-42. Friend, if we have knowledge, then should we teach that knowledge to others or not? If we should teach it, then what might be the thinking of people all over the world about it? Tell us in some detail?

Answer - Dear friend, knowledge is the public property of the whole world. Knowledge should be shared with everyone. People all over the world have different types of advice regarding this question. People all over the world think about this in three ways, **such as -**

1. Most of the people in the world believe that the knowledge they have is their property only, why should they teach knowledge to others, they do not teach knowledge to others thinking that others will never surpass them by learning knowledge from them. And there are many people who die, and their knowledge also dies with them.

2. There are very few people in the world who think that if I teach the knowledge I have to others, then others will learn this knowledge and teach it to others, only then this knowledge will move forward and others will be benefited, so they try to spread their knowledge in the whole world.

3. My own personal belief is that the knowledge we have must be taught to others. If we are thinking that this knowledge is only our property then it

would be 100% wrong because if the person from whom we have learned the knowledge or who has taught us the knowledge is also like that. If we think that knowledge is his and only his property then why would he teach us knowledge? If he had not taught us knowledge then we would not be knowledgeable today or today we are not talking about knowledge. If you have knowledge then you must teach knowledge to others and take it forward. Only your masters and your name will move forward.

Note - By not teaching knowledge, knowledge never decreases, rather knowledge keeps increasing. If you have knowledge, then definitely teach that knowledge to others and earn the greatest virtue in the world.

Question-43. Friends, all over the world, around 95% of the children between the age of 13 to 19 years are those who feel very bad about their parents. Friend, what should the children of this age do so that they remain mentally enslaved to everyone and their parents throughout their life? May the children be happy?

Answer - Dear friend, the question is, you are a very serious tourist. This is a very important question. I ask you for this. I thank you. Dear friend, the age from 13 years to 19 years is very important and precious for children. If children are born in this age If things get worse than their whole life is ruined and if the children improve at this age, then their life is over. Friends can save the child by having the information given below to know about his life and are You can also make your new life successful yourself **such as -**

Come children, let us all together teach ourselves the lesson of truth.

Make your name shine in the whole world by following the path of truth.

By serving my parents, I have brought them happiness in life.

Let us all together save ourselves from lies and dishonesty.

Come children, let us all come together———-

Children's heart is a blank paper on which only the truth can be written.

Sit together and tell the true history to your children.

He tells lies that make children mental slaves. Save your children from lies.

By learning true things, children should teach true things to others also.

Come children, let us all come together——

If parents are liars, then children will also become liars.

If parents are truthful then children will also become truthful.

If parents are fighters, then children will also become fighters.

Parents should improve themselves and teach their children to improve themselves.

Come children, let us all come together——-

If parents are liars, then children will also become liars.

If parents are truthful then children will also become truthful.

If parents are fighters, then children will also become fighters.

Parents should improve themselves and teach their children to improve themselves.

Come children, let us all come together——-

Send your children to study with a teacher who is honest.

He himself has taught the truth; he should teach the truth to his children also.

If his own life is good then he should make his children also have a good life.

Make your children knowledgeable by finding a knowledgeable scholar teacher.

Come on children, let us all come together...

Don't make friends with those who teach you to lie.

Make friends children with those who teach you to speak the truth.

Children should become children just like the children they meet.

Find true friends and maintain true friendship.

Come children, let us all come together——

Parents are first and teachers are the first to teach children to speak the truth.

Explain this to children again and again, that lying ruins life.

Keep your children away from false and dishonest children and introduce them to truthful and honest children.

If you want to make your children great, then teach them the lesson of truth. Come on, children, let us all come together...

Let us all together raise our children to be truthful and honest.

Together, protect your children from liars and dishonest people.

All of you embrace your children with love.

Meghraj Singh requests you to explain everything lovingly to your children.

Question-44. Friend, there is a conscious power in the human mind. How can a person awaken that power and reveal a little about which people have awakened conscious power?

Answer - Dear friend, according to my personal experience, conscious power is awakened in three types of people. **Such as -**

1. A true person.
2. Inquisitive person
3. Cheating person

True person - When the conscious power of a true person is awake, then everything that comes out of his mouth is beneficial and beneficial for the whole world, and he does good work for the whole world and tries to spread truth and honesty in the whole world. He does this work continuously, due to which people all over the world benefit a lot.

Inquisitive person - Searching person is not the time when the conscious power has awakened, at that time he starts trying to discover the things of the world. This includes many people like scientists, doctors, engineers and many other true people who make a difference in the world by searching something or the other. Create new inventions which greatly benefit the people of the world.

Cheating Person - People who cheat are the most dangerous people in the world. They are more dangerous than thieves and robbers. When thieves and robbers become corrupt, then they become thugs who fool the people of the world in the name of religion and keep looting from birth to death and also in the name of dead people. These thugs keep robbing their families and trap other people's mind in mental diseases. Such thugs spread mental slavery in the world, due to which billions and trillions of people of the world suffer huge losses.

If the swindlers accept truth and honesty wholeheartedly, then their awakened consciousness will

The power will be useful.

If the conscious power of thugs works properly in the world, then billions and trillions of people will be saved.

Mental slavery will end.

Those ordinary people who sometimes lie and sometimes tell the truth, their conscious power will never be awakened.

If ordinary people adopt truth and honesty wholeheartedly, their conscious power will also awaken.

Those whose conscious power has awakened and are working properly will see the whole world as their own.

Then the blessings of God, Allah, God, Waheguru will be upon those true people forever.

The fire of greed, hatred and evil will be extinguished from within those whose conscious power is working in the right direction.

By the grace of Meghraj Singh, Guru, those true people will truly attain supreme happiness.

Question-45. Friend, please tell us clearly about the theist, atheist and realist, what is the mental condition of the theist, atheist and realist?

Answer - Dear friend, about the theist, atheist and realist, I want to tell you in detail **such as -**

- Those people who blindly follow religion without thinking, we call them theists.

- Those people who reject religion without thinking, we call them atheists.

- We call those who seek a religion based on truth as genuine.

Theist - Today's theists are those people who have accepted religion blindly and have been considering religion as a tradition. Today's theists are those people who do not have much knowledge of religion, and today they are sitting as contractors of religion. And they have not given the correct knowledge of religion to the people, rather they have enslaved almost 90% of the people by wrapping them in faith, due to which people have neither been able to understand the religion, nor have they been able to understand the religious traditions, nor have they been able to learn humanity from the religion. If theists are sometimes telling the truth and sometimes lying, then these people can never have true knowledge of religion.

Atheists - today's atheists are those people who were once very religious. These people followed the traditions of religion on the advice of others. They continued to follow religion and believed in the beliefs of religion. They continued to believe in God, but today they have stopped believing in God on the advice of other Someone else said. Is it that God is not in the world or God has not created the world due to which he has left the religion and separated himself, now he has become an atheist, he never used his mind that earlier religion was dependent on someone else's advice, today he has left the religion and gone away, that too for someone else. But if atheists had accepted truth and honesty as religion, they would never have left religion. The atheist who does not know about truth and honesty or the atheist who sometimes tells the truth and sometimes lies will never know about religion and the one who cannot know about truth and honesty will never know about God, Allah, Waheguru, god. Will be able to know because truth is God and God is truth. One who does not know about truth will never be able to know about God.

Real - Real people we call those who really live life in the right way or search about life or identify right and wrong. Only real man can identify religion and only real man can discover truth and honesty. Because a real person never accepts anything blindly, he searches for that thing and only those people who search are successful. We call those people real who can achieve anything on the basis of truth and honesty. Those who search or search for religion become successful. The search for truth and honesty is the search for religion, hence only real people can recognize religion in the right way.

Only if theists and atheists adopt truth and honesty will they be able to recognize reality.

Only if theists and atheists search for truth and honesty, they will be able to recognize religion correctly.

Only real people are true and honest, and they spread truth and honesty in the whole world.

Meghraj Singh accepts the whole world as his family because of his courage and honesty.

Question-46. Friend, there is a population of about 7.5 billion people in the whole world. None of them have seen God till date. What is the reason behind this? Please tell us clearly.

Answer - Dear friend, your question is very valid, and it should also be asked that there is a population of approximately 7.5 billion people in the world, why have none of them had the darshan of God till date? I will try to explain the answer to this question by giving you worldly examples, such as -

Number one - Like we use a mobile phone, the waves in the SIM card come from the tower. By looking at the tower, we can find out that it is a tower, but we cannot detect the waves coming from the tower, but we can see those waves through a telescope or any other means.

Number two - When there is pain in a person's body, a person can not only feel the pain but cannot see it with his eyes. If it is shown through binoculars or a computer, then we can see it, that is, the pain will not be visible with the eyes but will be felt. Have to do it.

Number three - As if there is a fragrance coming from the flower, but what color is the fragrance of the flower, whether it is black or white, no one can tell what color it is, rather the fragrance can be felt, but it cannot be told what color the fragrance is.

Number four - Like air oxygen, which most of the people call wind, we are breathing with this oxygen, but what color is it, what is it, where is it coming from, we can almost see it with binoculars or any other means, but it is not visible with eyes, we can only feel it. Are

Number five - Just as we can see till the sky with our eyes, we can see till far away, but we are never able to see the light of our eyes, what color is the light of our eyes, whether it is black, white or yellow.

God can only be felt, He cannot be seen.

The one who has found God is not even able to tell what shape God is or what form God is in.

What color is it? Only one can know its qualities.

Such as the world example

Number One - For example, if we have a drop of water and if we mix it in the ocean, will that drop of water come back to tell us what is the size of the ocean? That drop of water can never tell how big is the size of the ocean. Nor can we take that drop of water back.

Number Two - As you all must have seen the waves rising in the sea, humans see those waves and feel happy seeing them, but those waves can never tell how big is the size of the sea.

- Just as there is an ocean, there are also waves.

- In the same way, if there is a God, then there are also human beings.

Number three - Just like the sun's rays are connected to the sun, but the sun's rays can never tell how big the sun is or what the sun is like, it can only give light to others.

- Just like there is sun, there are rays too.

- In the same way, if God exists then he is also a human being.

Number four - Like there is a seed, inside the seed there is a tree and inside the tree there is a seed. It is like a tree has to take the support of the earth to produce seeds, and the earth gives many times more seeds than that.

Like the seed is hidden inside the tree and the tree is hidden inside the seed.
Similarly, God is hidden inside humans and living beings and all living beings and humans are hidden inside God.

A person who has lies and dishonesty inside him will not be able to understand this.
Only the person who has truth and honesty will be able to understand this.

The people who are broken from God are the ones
who believe in the caste and caste system.
The people who are connected to God are the ones
who do not believe in caste or caste system.

The person who is broken from God is the one who
hates people in the name of racism, in the name of
caste.
The person who is connected to God is the one who
rises above all the differences of appearance, caste
and creed and loves everyone.

The identity of a person who is broken from God is
that his mind is mine, his body and money are mine
too.
The identity of a person who is connected to God is
that the mind is yours, your body and your wealth
are also yours.

A person who has lies and dishonesty inside him
will not be able to understand this.
Only the person who has truth and honesty will be
able to understand this.

The people who are broken from God are the ones
who believe in the caste and caste system.
The people who are connected to God are the ones
who do not believe in caste or caste system.

The person who is broken from God is the one who hates people in the name of racism, in the name of caste.

The person who is connected to God is the one who rises above all the differences of appearance, caste and creed and loves everyone.

The identity of a person who is broken from God is that his mind is mine, his body and money are mine too.

The identity of a person who is connected to God is that the mind is yours, your body and your wealth are also yours.

Question-47. Friend, many people have this question that why have we come into this world, or why has God sent us to earth or have we come into this world just to have fun? What is your opinion about this question?

Answer - Dear friend, why has man come into this world or why has God sent man to this earth, this is the question of almost 99% of people. Let us all together find the answer to this question. **Such as -**

There are many names of the same God, which people call Bhagwan, Vaheguhe Ru, Allah, God or remember the name of the same God in their own way.

Allah, God, Bhagwan, Waheguru, which are many names of the same power, are born and die under the orders of the living beings of the entire world.

Only one God created the entire universe. He has created many living beings in this universe who come and go to provide happiness to each other. Birth and death are natural processes. Fate has nothing to do with it.

Whatever God has created or has created, death will definitely come. Whatever God has created in this world is one, it has been created to bring happiness to others, as if

Wind - Wind is giving breath to the living beings of the entire universe.

Earth - providing food to the people of the world, fruits and vegetables and remaining a home for them.

Water - is quenching the thirst of living beings throughout the universe.

Fire - Fire is used for cooking food.

Petrol Diesel - Used to drive vehicles.

Gold and silver adorn the necks of men and women.

Sun - Energy is spreading throughout the universe from the Sun.

All types of trees and plants that have been born on this earth are for the benefit of all.

Like animals and birds are eating each other, then it is a law of nature, by doing this they are eating each other, otherwise all the living beings, animals and

birds, apart from humans, help each other and die after passing their life in this world.

In this world, human beings have been sent to help each other and to bring happiness, but the environment in which a person gets, **he becomes like that. Is such as -**

one has become a believer,

Third forest has gone blindly

the other has become an atheist,

the fourth has become aware

Theist - The one who gets such an environment becomes a theist, in that environment, religious lessons are taught, religious books are memorized, and it is also told that after death, one will get heaven and hell, one will get heaven and hell. These names create greed among the people and Fear set in, and those people were afraid of the name of God and continued to walk sheepishly throughout their lives in fear, then while walking like this, they died without living a life of freedom.

Atheist - Atheist is the one who got such an environment that his companions or other people told him that God does not exist in this world and there is no need of God. God did not create humans. It is a law of nature. He left God and went away and started religion. He also left and turned away from religion.

Blind devotees - Blind devotees became those who found such an environment that if someone said that they have to worship graves, they worshiped the graves. If someone said that they have to worship idols, then they worshiped idols. And if anyone said anything, they did the same. If someone said that stealing brings peace, then they stole. That if someone said that chanting the name gives peace, then he chanted the name, he did everything only on the advice of others, he never used his mind, he remained a blind devotee throughout his life, he never got peace in his life.

Aware - A wise person became the one who got such an environment, he got true and honest people, he got people who showed the path of truth and honesty, he accepted the truth and searched for the truth, and he also came to know that God, Allah, or God is within him. , He is God and he has benefited the people. Have I brought happiness to the people? And happiness is reached only by those who have happiness within themselves.

As you do, you will be filled, this is the law of nature.

A person will get the result according to his karma.

If you do bad, you will get sorrow and will spend your whole life in sorrow.

If you do good, you will get happiness and your whole life will be spent in happiness.

Those who do bad look happy on the outside, but are very sad on the inside.

Those who do good look simple on the outside, but are happy on the inside.

Those who do bad things become plotters, corrupt, rapists and villains.

Those who do good work become charitable, philanthropic, virtuous and great.

What is the order of God?

- Speaking the truth and propagating the truth is the command of God.

- To work honestly and to teach others to work honestly is also God's command.

- Working hard for your career and achieving success is also God's order.

- It is also God's order to eat bread after working hard and not to eat it by asking others in the name of God.

- It is also God's command not to trap people in the greed for heaven and heaven.

- It is also God's order not to scare people with the name of hell and hell.

- Not to hate others in the name of caste and religion is also God's command.

- It is also God's command to consider the people of the entire world as members of your family.

- Spreading truth throughout the world and eradicating hatred is also God's order.

- Teaching a lesson to the enemy and embracing poor people is also God's order.

Note - Dear friend, only a true and honest person can understand this important information.

Question-48. Friends, what are the things people around the world think that cause harm to themselves mentally and physically?

Answer: Dear friend, if the people of the world **think such as -**

1. I am the best person in the world, everyone else in front of me are insects and animals.

2. Only I can do everything in this world, no one else.

3. I am the most knowledgeable person in this world, everyone else is ignorant.

4. I am the tallest man, this is black, this is brown, this is all my white faces.

5. I have come into this world to live freely, everyone else has remained my slave.

6. I remain the most powerful in this world and everyone else remains weak.

7. I will become the richest person in the world and everyone else will remain poor.

8. Everyone respect me, I keep insulting everyone.

9. Even if I lie, be dishonest, commit corruption or do any wrong in the world, I am still the highest.

10. I had done a lot of good work in my previous birth, that is why I was born in a high caste or high race family. I am the best in the world and I am a god.

If any person in the world thinks like this, then all the good qualities will die out of him, then only bad qualities will arise in him, due to which hatred will arise in him, then his whole life will keep burning in the fire of hatred and others will also get the fire of hatred. One person who burns in the fire of hatred will burn crores of people in the fire of hatred.

The examples given above are very serious and dangerous mental problems for humans.

The easiest solution to this problem... Those who accept the truth wholeheartedly will be saved from all these problems and hatred will end from within them.

Truth will generate love, humanity, patience, satisfaction and kindness in them which will make their life blissful.

Question-49. Friends, what are the things people around the world think about that benefit themselves mentally and physically?

Answer - Dear friend, if the people of the world think like this then it will be 100% beneficial for **them such as**

1. I have come into this world, there are millions of people like me who have also come into this world.

2. As I am a human being, I am a human being in the entire world. We are all human and equal.

3. If I am knowledgeable, then all human beings become knowledgeable and no human being remains unintelligent in this world.

4. If I am living a very comfortable life by eating bread, then O Lord, please give a similar life to the people of the whole world.

5. No human being in the entire world is black. Some are fair, some are brown, we are all created by one God, all are equal.

6. We all have the same flesh and blood, we are all people of the whole world, we are not different.

7. No religion is small or big. Religion is the name of truth and honesty. If there is truth and honesty in all religions then all religions are equal.

8. No one is of high caste, no one is of low caste, no one is of high caste, no one is of low caste, we are all children of the same God.

9. For me truth and honesty is religion and for me lies and dishonesty are religion.

10. For me, the whole world is my family. There is only one God among the animals and humans of the whole world, that is why I love everyone.

If a person thinks like this then he will attain supreme knowledge from within himself due to which love only love, humanity only humanity, kindness only kindness will come within him. He will love everyone equally and will teach everyone to live with love.

Love is born from truth, only the person who has love inside him can love the people of the whole world.

Love is life, love is humanity, only through love can happiness arise and only through love can one find a loving God.

Note - If even the liars and dishonest people truly keep the truth in their mind, then love will develop in them too, and they will also get supreme happiness and will also find a loving God.

Question-50. Friend, who do you consider to be the most powerful person in the world?

Answer - Dear friend, according to my personal experience, I consider the one who spreads truth and honesty in the world and raises voice in favor of the poor and oppressed **to be the most powerful, such as -**

A true person is the most powerful in the entire world.

- Whether a true man has money or wealth or not, he is still powerful.

- Whether a liar has money or wealth or not, he is still weak. A true person is the most powerful in the entire world.

- Even if a true man has no wealth at all, he is still the most powerful person in the world.

- Even if a liar has all the wealth in the world, he is still the weakest person in the world.

- True people can easily improve even the most difficult tasks of the world.

- Liars spoil even the simplest tasks of the world.

- Even the most difficult tasks appear easy to a true person.

- To a liar, even the simplest of tasks appear difficult.

- If you want to do the work, then every work is easy for you.

- If you do not want to do the work, then every work is difficult for you.

- If even false people adopt the truth, they will also become powerful.

- He will then be able to do even the most difficult tasks in the world with ease.

- Only a true person is powerful, he becomes fearless of Yamraj and the fear of death.

- Meghraj Singh, the name of a true man, is remembered for centuries in the world.

Question-51. Friend, this question arises again and again in the minds of many people that who should they make as their role model? Please clarify a little about this?

Answer - Dear friend, if we or the people of the world want to make someone our role model, then we can choose our role model by reading the examples given below **carefully, such as -**

- If we make any leader, leader of any organization, any film actor, any businessman or any beautiful girl or boy our role model, then we will never be able to succeed and will also forget our identity.

- If we do not make a politician, a leader, a film actor, a businessman or a beautiful girl or boy our role model but instead make truth and honesty our role model, then we will be 100% successful in our life and will be able to make our mark in the world.

Note - Whoever makes truth and honesty his role model, one day he himself will become a role model for others and will shine in the world.

Question-52. Friend, you must be aware that people all over the world fear the name of hell and hell and run after the greed of heaven and heaven. Friend, tell us in detail where is hell, and where is heaven?

Answer - Dear friend, almost 90% of the people in the whole world believe that hell, hell, heaven and heaven are not above this earth, they are somewhere else, but according to my personal experience, this earth is hell and hell for those who lie. This earth is heaven and paradise for those who speak the truth, **such as -**

Where is hell?

1. If we lie and are dishonest, our body will become like hell.

2. If the entire family lies and is dishonest, then the entire family is like hell.

3. If the entire village lies and is dishonest, then the entire village will be like hell.

4. If the people of the entire state lie and act dishonestly, then the entire state will be like hell.

5. If the people of the entire country lie and act dishonestly, then the entire country will be like hell.

6. If people all over the world lie and are dishonest then the whole world will be like hell.

Where is heaven?

1. If we speak the truth and live honestly, our body itself is like heaven.

2. If the entire family speaks the truth and is honest, then the entire family is like heaven.

3. If the entire village speaks the truth and is honest, then the entire village is like heaven.

4. If the people of the entire state speak the truth and are honest, then the entire state will be like heaven.

5. If the people of the entire country speak the truth and are honest, then the entire country will be like heaven.

6. If people all over the world speak the truth and are honest, then the whole world will be like heaven.

Poetry
After death, some will go to heaven and some will go to hell.

This is all imaginary thought.

Looting wealth from living people by misleading them is a trap spread by Satan. Those who are not afraid will burn in the fire of fear all their lives in Hell. Those who are greedy for heaven will remain greedy and wander throughout their lives.

The person who accepts the truth wholeheartedly will be free from the fear of hell and

The greed for heaven will end.

He will remain happy all the time and his life will become like heaven.

Only a true and honest person will spread the truth throughout the world and make the whole world like heaven.

Meghraj Singh Only a true person will find his beloved Lord from within himself with love.

Note - Any person in the whole world who will give up lies and adopt the truth from his heart will be able to make himself and the whole world like heaven.

Question-53. Friends, we all have five disorders within us. Let us know a little about the advantages and disadvantages of the five disorders.

Tell us about so that we can learn some words of wisdom?

Answer - Dear friend, if five disorders remain under the control of a person, then only benefits are brought to him and if five disorders go out of the control of a person, then only harm is caused to him, **such as -**

Lust, anger, greed, attachment, ego and pride are five vices. If they are limited, then they give only happiness to a person.

Lust, anger, greed, attachment, ego and pride are five vices. If they go out of their limits, then they bring only sorrow to a person.

If the five vices remain under control, they are of great benefit to man.

If these five vices go out of control, they cause great harm to humans.

If lusted, anger, greed, attachment, ego are kept under control, then what benefits will they bring to humans? Let us know -

Work- If the lust of lust remains under control, then the person will remain limited to his family and will feel relaxed in life only with his family and will create his own family with his life partner and his mind will not wander.

Anger - If anger remains under control, then a person will neither harm himself nor harm others, it will benefit that person.

Greed - Greed is a distorted form of greed. If a person's greed or avarice remains under control, then the person will earn and eat the bread of his hard work for his family and will be happy.

Attachment -If attachment remain under control, then a person will nurture his family very lovingly and will also maintain his relatives and will never run away from his family.

Ego - If ego is controlled then it will take the form of self-respect due to which a person will fight against oppression and will also raise his voice against oppression and will remain happy.

If lusted, anger, greed, attachment, ego go out of a person's control, then what harm will they cause to a person, let us know.

Work -If a man's sexual desire goes out of control, it takes a very dangerous form. If a man's sexual desire goes out of control, even if he has relations with women from all over the world, his sexual desire will not be quenched. If a woman's sexual desire goes out of control, even if she has relations with men from all over the world, her sexual desire will not be quenched. This makes a person's mind go astray and his life gets completely ruined.

Anger - If anger goes out of a person's control, then due to anger, a person commits big crimes, commits murder, ruins his own life and also ruins the lives of others. The biggest loss that a person causes due to this is himself. It happens.it happens

Greed - Greed is a distorted form of greed. If a person's greed goes out of control, then the person becomes so ferocious, so terrible, so dangerous that he kills any person for the sake of wealth and gets many big murders done. Even if a person has all the wealth and gold and silver in the world, his greed will never end, and his life gets completely ruined in this process.

Attachment - Attachment is a distorted form of love. If attachment goes out of a person's control, then due to attachment, a person can take the lives of others or can even give up his own life. Attachment is so dangerous that to fulfill one's wish, a person does everything. Attachment that crosses limits causes greater harm to a person's own self.

Egoism - If egoism goes out of control in a person, it gives birth to anger. Egoism sets such a fire of hatred in a person's life that he never cares about the harm of others and also cares about his own harm. He does not do this; he causes great harm. Sometimes such a person commits many murders and even goes to jail. Such a person ruins his own life with his own hands.

If lusted, anger, greed, attachment, ego go out of control, a person will become a devil. If a person remains trapped in lust, anger, greed, attachment and ego, he will remain an ordinary person.

If one understands lust, anger, greed, attachment and ego then a person will become a scholar.

If one can control lust, anger, greed, attachment and ego then a person will become great.

If one controls lust, anger, greed, attachment and ego and inculcates the truth in one's mind, one will attain ultimate knowledge from within.

By the grace of Meghraj Singh Guru, the name of the one who controls lust, anger, greed, attachment and ego will continue for as long as this world exists.

Note - The person who will inculcate truth and honesty in his mind will be free from lust, anger, greed, attachment and ego in life itself.

Question- 54. Friend, if there is any kind of fear inside a person, then what is the benefit and harm to the person due to fear?

Answer - Dear friend, fear does not benefit a person at all, **rather it only causes loss.**

Such as -

Fear is a mental illness, avoid it...

- If there is fear in the mind, a person can die even from an insect bite.
- If there is no fear in the mind then even an elephant cannot kill a person.
- If there is fear in the mind then a person may die even from the bite of a small snake.
- If there is no fear in the mind, then even the python cannot do any harm to the human being.

- If there is fear in the mind then the person may die from a virus.
- If there is no fear in the mind then even thousands of viruses cannot kill a person.
- If there is fear in the mind then one should run away in fear even from a human insect.
- If there is no fear in the mind then a person can even collide with an elephant.
- If there is fear in the mind then even a devil can kill a person.
- If there is no fear in the mind then millions of devils will run away in fear.
- The devils scare the humans who are afraid day and night.
- Those people who are not afraid, devils salute them day and night.
- Those who are afraid of themselves scare others too.
- Those who are fearless make others fearless.
- Those who scare others are the devils on this earth.
- Meghraj Singh: Only the one who embraces the poor is great on this earth.

Note - Whoever accepts the truth wholeheartedly, his fear will disappear forever and then he will live a happy life without any fear.

Question-55. Friend, you are talking very big about humanism and you also try to call the people of the whole world as your family members. What work have you done to show the people of the world the

path of truth which can help the people of the whole world? Can people live a life of peace and brotherhood by following the path of truth?

Answer - Dear friend, according to the ability and wealth that Waheguru has given me, I have prepared a song in 25 languages of the world which will bring peace and tranquility in the whole world and people of the world can live their lives happily by following the path of truth. I want to tell you in full detail about the languages in which we have prepared this song and the purpose for **which we have prepared it, such as -**

Message of peace for the whole world...

Respected, my dear family members from all over the world, it is a matter of great happiness for all of you that we have prepared a song in 25 languages of the world which will spread the message of truth and honesty in the whole world. This song has solutions to the problems of the whole world.

I have written this song with the grace of Guru; the lyrics of the song are as follows.

Why should humans become enemies of humans? Everyone should think.

A dilemma has arisen which we all must resolve.

1. English
2. Punjabi
3. Arabic
4. Pashtu
5. Gujarati

6. Rajasthani
7. Bhojpuri
8. Korea
9. Afghani
10. Persian (Farsi)
11. Urdu
12. Bengali
13. Chinese
14. Japanese
15. Spanish
16. French
17. German
18. Indonesian
19. Nepali
20. Turkish
21. Romanian
22. Italian
23. Russian
24. Hindi
25. Haryanvi

Why have we made this song in 25 languages of the world?

We have prepared this song in 25 languages of the world because when we got attention all over the world

If we have seen from the past, we have seen darkness of ignorance all around and we have seen almost 90% of the people of the world trapped in mental slavery.

One country is fighting with another country. One person is killing another person. In the name of caste, in the name of religion, in the name of race, one person is shedding the blood of another person. So when we saw all these problems, we thought that lies, dishonesty and greed are behind the situation that has arisen all over the world.

When we saw people fighting among themselves, two countries fighting among themselves, we saw lies and dishonesty behind it. It is because of lies and dishonesty that people are fighting among themselves, so we have prepared this song in 25 languages. There is a solution to the whole world's problems.

What is our motive behind making this song?

My aim behind making this song is that the people of the world should live life with love and consider each other as their own. This song has a tempo and 6 stanzas. There are 6 differences in three lines each. In two lines we have mentioned the problems and in the third line we have given the solutions to the problems.

Why has this song been prepared in 25 languages?

We have prepared this song in 25 languages because when we read the words of Guru Nanak Sahib Ji, we came to know that all happiness arises from truth and all sorrows arise from lies, then when lies arise sorrows and truth Happiness will arise then we have decided to spread truth and honesty all over the world through this song because we have prepared this song in different languages so that people can adopt truth and honesty in their lives in their respective languages. I can feel happy and live life happily.

My personal interest behind making this song in 25 languages is this

Number one – People all over the world can live life with love and affection.

Number two – people all over the world can rise above racism and apartheid and live happy lives.

Number three – People all over the world can remove misconceptions and live a happy life.

Number four - People all over the world can rise above caste and religion and understand every human being as a human being.

Number five - People of the whole world can be saved from the fire of greed, dishonesty, lies and corruption.

Number six – People all over the world have been able to escape from rape, inferiority complex and pride.

Number seven – People all over the world, rich and poor, can live an equal life.

Number eight - People all over the world can be saved from mental diseases like jealousy, slander, backbiting and problems.

Number nine - People all over the world can live a life of truth, honesty, peace and patience, contentment.

Number ten - People all over the world can consider the whole world as their family and live life with love and one

Can live life by lovingly embracing others. Ever since we accepted the truth, every single person in the whole world started looking at us as our own. Lord Allah, God Waheguru, who is the only God, was seen sitting inside all the people of the entire world.

If any person in the world helps us with money or dollars to prepare this song in the languages of the whole world, then we will spread the message of truth to the entire humanity by preparing this song in the languages of the whole world. People can live a happy life full of peace and brotherhood.

Note - This is a humanitarian mission. People from all over the world can join this mission and can make their lives successful by following the path of truth and honesty. Contact us to join this mission

WhatsApp number +13474754233 USA

Question-56. Friends, why do wars happen within the world and how can wars be ended from within the world?

Answer - Dear friend, following are the reasons for wars in the world and if the people of the world adopt these rules, then **there will never be wars in the world. Such as -**

- Wars take place in the world only because of politics.
- World wars can end only because of politics.
- If political people all over the world are liars and dishonest then one day there will definitely be wars.

- If political people all over the world are truthful and honest then there will never be wars in the world.
- If political people are liars and deceitful then they will harm the country to benefit themselves.
- If political people are truthful and honest, they will benefit themselves and also benefit the countrymen.
- If political people all over the world are liars and dishonest then they will take away the peace of the whole world and its people.
- If political people all over the world are true and honest then they will establish peace in the whole world.

What is the reason behind why there are wars in the world?

1. If politics or political power will be in the hands of dishonest and liars.
2. If there will be corrupt and rapist people in politics.
3. If there will be greedy, greedy and bitter speaking people in politics.
4. If there will be arrogant, angry and worthless people in politics.
5. If the conspirators in politics are treacherous and cunning people.

So war will definitely happen one day.

Who benefits from war and who suffers loss?

1. War benefits 2% of political devils.

2. War causes loss to 98% of the population.

What is the mental state of those who fight wars?

1. The mental state of those who wage war is like that of slaves, that is why they work to enslave others also.
2. The mental state of those instigating war is like that of madmen and greedy dogs.

What harm do those who wage war do to themselves?

1. If wars are being waged to enslave others, then they are wasting their precious time, money, dollars, mental strength and physical strength.
2. In the process of enslaving others, he will not be able to live peacefully even for a moment because first he will waste his energy in enslaving others and then he will enslave them forever.
3. They will waste their precious time in keeping them slaves due to which they will not be able to live comfortably even for a day.

How can wars in the world be ended? If the people of the world follow these rules, then there will never be wars in the world. Such as -

1. If political or political power will be in the hands of true and honest people.
2. If politics will be in the hands of virtuous and charitable people.
3. If politics will be in the hands of people with clean intentions and sweet speaking people.
4. If politics will be in the hands of people with patience, contentment and tolerance.

5. If politics will be in the hands of humanitarian and egalitarian people.

So, there will never be wars in the world.

Who will benefit and who will be harmed by not going to war?

1. 98% people in the world will benefit and get happiness.
2. 2% of the people of the world will feel that they are facing loss because their greed will not be satisfied but they will also benefit because greed will be eliminated from within them because greed is the root of all troubles.

What will be the mental condition of those who do not fight?

1. The mental state of people who do not fight is one of freedom.
2. People who are free themselves give others the right to live freely, due to which even politicians and people of the country live peacefully.

If they do not fight, they save themselves from any loss.

1. If the issues of war are being resolved through talks, then they are saving their money, dollars, mental strength, physical strength and their precious time from getting wasted.
2. The people who resolve big wars through negotiations, both themselves and their countrymen live a peaceful life.

Poetry: Attacks on innocents are illegitimate.

It is permissible to teach a lesson to the culprit.

The real powerful are not those who dominate the innocent.

Attack children.

The real powerful are those who destroy the perpetrators of crimes.

Fight for the rights of the poor and the oppressed.

Note - Only intelligent, knowledgeable, powerful and fearless people work for the happiness of the country and its people and give them the right to live with complete freedom and live their lives in complete happiness.

Friend, thank you very much for answering my questions very seriously.

Dear friend, you have also asked even more serious questions about the mysterious things in the mind about slavery. Very few people think about these issues. Thank you very much for asking questions on these issues.

Poetry: Do not befriend a false person

If a false person is your friend, then he will be more dangerous than the enemy.

From outside that trust may be trustworthy but from inside that trust will be fatal.

If a friend praises you falsely then that praise can become an obstacle for the person's mind.

If your friend is a liar then that flattery can be fatal for a person.

False praise creates pride in a person's mind.

Pride becomes a hindrance in the development of human mind.

Flattery makes a person cowardly and weak from within.

Cowardice and weakness become fatal for a person himself.

If friends teach you to lie, then that lie will lead to destruction.

If friends teach you to be dishonest then problems may arise due to dishonesty.

If friends teach us to be rapists and abusers, then the friends themselves become like enemies.

If friends teach us to commit corruption and atrocities, then friends become more dangerous than enemies.

If your friend praises you for something false as well as true.

Such a friend can be selfish, stay away from such a friend.

Be friends with a friend who stops you from lying and teaches you to tell the truth.

Even if such a friend scold you for committing a mistake, still maintain your friendship with truth.

Friendship is the sweetest relationship, maintain friendship with truth, honesty and love.

Meghraj Singh came together in happiness and sorrow to help each other and created a new history in the world.

Poetry: Make friendship with a true person

Make friendship with a true person, it will help you in happiness and sorrow.

He will maintain friendship with complete truth and honesty throughout his life.

The one who stops us from doing bad deeds is called a true friend.

The one who inspires us to do good work is called a true friend.

The one who stops one from lying and being dishonest is called a true friend.

The one who stops us from committing corruption, rape and misconduct is called a true friend.

The one who stops people from stealing and cheating is called a true friend.

The one who stops good people from criticizing or gossiping is called a true friend.

The one who stands by us truthfully in bad times is called a true friend.

The one who shows the way to avoid misconceptions is called a true friend.

The one who explains that people of all religions are equal is called a true friend.

The one who explains that people all over the world are ours is called a true friend.

Truth and honesty are religion. The one who tells this is called a true friend.

The one who teaches us to work honestly is called a true friend.

One who himself follows the path of truth and honesty and shows the path of truth to others also.

A true friend is the one who remains friends in happiness as well as in sorrow.

The friendship of a true friend is remembered for centuries in the world.

Meghraj Singh: Friendship of truth and honesty becomes an example in the world.

Poem: The path of lies is painful

The path of lies is very painful, protect yourself from
it.

It is because of lies that a person gets trapped in the
quagmire of mental sorrows.

It is because of lies that a person starts telling lies
day and night.

Only lies can make a person commit dishonest acts
day and night.

Only lies can make people indulge in corruption day
and night.

Only lies can make a person coward and coward from
within.

To eliminate their fear, humans should kill others.

Only lies can make people buy lawyers and judges
again.

He is a liar and then calls himself a capable person.

Only a liar can fool people by telling lies.

When liars sit among themselves and start talking.

Calling yourself great and calling people great fools.

It is because of lies that man becomes a devil and a
devil.

To keep himself happy, he should cause pain to
others.

Liars are slaves from within, that is why they enslave others.

Slave people are full of sorrows, that is why they cause sorrow to others.

Lies are the root of all sorrows, protect yourself from lies.

Truth is the root of all happiness. Adopt the truth from your heart.

Make life happy by abandoning lies and adopting truth in your life.

By the grace of Meghraj Singh Guru, attain ultimate happiness within yourself through true knowledge.

Poem: The path of truth is pleasant

The path of truth is happiness; keep the truth in your mind.

It is only because of truth that man can come out of the quagmire of slavery.

Only truth should save man from greed and dishonesty.

Only truth can save man from corruption and committing crimes.

Only the truth should save humans from misbehavior, rape and torture.

Only truth should save man from inequality, evil and brutality.

Only truth can take a person out of the gutter of caste and caste system.

Only truth should save man from hatred of high and low and discrimination.

Only truth should save man from apartheid and racism.

Only the truth can eradicate the hatred of apartheid and racism from within humans.

Only truth can eliminate mental slavery from within a person.

Only truth can liberate man from mental slavery.

Only truth makes a person learned, wise and great.

Only truth makes a person virtuous, characterful and honest.

Truth alone makes a person charitable, courageous and strong.

Only truth can make a person compassionate, powerful and fearless.

Only a true person should embrace the poor, the oppressed and the destitute.

Only a true person should teach a lesson to enemies, demons and devils.

Only a true person should spread truth and honesty in the whole world.

Only a true person can understand that the whole world is one family.

True God, Allah Waheguru, make man in the form of God.

By the grace of Meghraj Singh Guru, a true person gets ultimate happiness.

Some very important and amazing information.

Truth is the rain of happiness which extinguishes the fire of greed and desires from within.

Truth is an ocean of pleasures which quenches the thirst of lust from within.

Truth is the light of knowledge which eradicates the ignorance of hypocrisy from within.

Truth is the lamp of knowledge which burns the ignorance of lies from within.

Truth is a river of love that can wash away hatred and jealousy from life.

Truth is the name of trust and belonging which removes duplicity from within.

Truth is humanity and equality which should eradicate evil and inequality from within.

Truth is the bulldozer of love that can demolish the walls of casteism, racism and caste system.

Truth is an ocean of happiness which absorbs all types of sorrows within itself and leads to supreme happiness.

Meghraj Singh: The treasure of true happiness can be found only by the one who is blessed by his Guru.

Note - The person who is true from inside as well as from outside, the Guru is happy with him and blesses him with the treasure of true happiness due to which the life of the person becomes supremely happy and blissful.

Poem: Truth is like nectar for man, lie is like poison for man

Nectar gives life to a human being and poison gives death to the human body.

Like food and water are beneficial for the human body.

Similarly, truth and honesty are beneficial for the human mind.

Like poison and any intoxicant is harmful for the human body.

Similarly, lies and dishonesty are harmful for the human mind.

Like good food and good water keeps the body healthy.

Similarly, truth and honesty keep the mind healthy.

For example, human health deteriorates due to bad food and bad water.

Similarly, mental health deteriorates due to lies and dishonesty.

Like good food and good water keeps the human body alive.

Similarly, a person's conscience remains alive with truth and honesty.

Just as poison causes death to the human body.

Similarly, lies kill a person's conscience.

For example, if a person has light in the dark of night, then he can save his body from many troubles.

Similarly, if a person's mind has true knowledge, then he can save his mind from many troubles.

For example, if a person does not have any arrangement for light at night, then the person gets lost in the dark.

Similarly, if a person does not have the light of true knowledge, then the mind wanders in the darkness of ignorance.

Just as good food and good water bring happiness to the human body.

Similarly, the human mind gets only happiness from the true knowledge of true great men.

Just like bad food and bad water will bring only sorrow to the human body.

Similarly, lies and dishonesty will only bring sorrow to the human mind.

Just as a person's body becomes strong with good food and good water.

Similarly, a person's mind becomes strong only through truth and honesty.

For example, human body becomes weak due to bad food and bad water.

Similarly, a person's mind becomes weak due to lies and dishonesty.

The person who continuously consumes good food and good water, his body will remain healthy forever.

Those people who will continuously walk on the path of truth and honesty,

The mind will always be healthy.

If the mind is healthy then the body is also healthy. Only when the mind and body are healthy.

Man's life will be happy.

Truth will give birth to good qualities, patience, contentment, peace and happiness, then human life will be filled with happiness.

Will become rich from.

For a person whose mind is dry and his body is dry, the whole world will be his family.

By the grace of Meghraj Singh Guru, that person's life will become blissful and happy.

Note - Whoever embraces truth and honesty wholeheartedly will attain this wonderful and important Will be able to understand knowledge and live life in bliss.

Note

How will people all over the world live a free life? All the topics we have given our views on in this book are related to the lives of people all over the world. Almost all the issues related to human freedom and slavery are written in these thoughts. We have tried our best to make these thoughts clear and put them in front of all of you so that you can learn something from them and teach something to your people, your family, your society. Try these ideas. We know that many people may agree or disagree. If any question has arisen in your mind after reading these ideas, then contact us on our WhatsApp number.

We want to see the whole world happy, we want to see it living in freedom, when man is free then only the country will be happy and when the country is happy then the whole world will be happy.

The world will be happy, the day true and honest youth from different countries of the world come into politics and enter the Parliament, that day the whole world will be happy. I can say this with hope and I also hope that the youth of the whole world will become like this. Will definitely make the day and make the whole world happy.

My personal WhatsApp number +13474754233 USA

Thoughts

We all have come into this world like travelers and one day or the other we all have to leave this world and after that we all will be at our home, the home which we will get in return for our good deeds and till then why don't we stay together. Be a support to others and cheer for each other. Don't compare your life with someone else's life. We all are a unique creation of the Almighty. Don't criticize anyone, don't hate anyone. We were created to love everyone for who they are. It is better to make a person happy than to criticize him. Spread love and harmony wherever we go. I congratulate Meghraj Singh on writing this book.

Christina Evers
Public Motivational Speaker, Social Influencer

My name is Nicola Lettero, I live in America. I have read many of these articles written by Meghraj Singh. He writes absolutely true things. Whatever is written in this book, whoever reads it will be freed from mental slavery. I am proud of writing this book. I congratulate Meghraj Singh for this.

Nicola Lettero (USA)

I am Dharam Singh from Australia. I have known Meghraj Singh since 1997. He has been my student. He had taken the path of truth and honesty since that time, and today he has written this book named "How the people of the whole world Live your life freely" In this book, he has exposed a lot of truth. Whoever reads this book will get a lot of benefit. I congratulate Meghraj Singh very much for writing this book.

Dharam Singh (Australia)

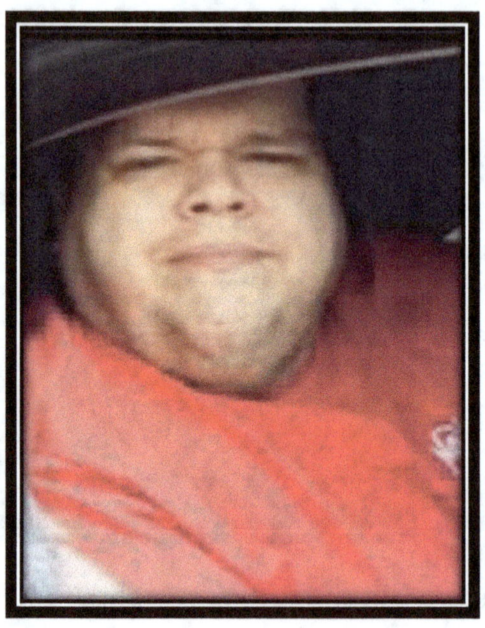

My name is Frankie I am from America. The path of truth is the only one that can free man from mental slavery. Whoever reads this book will become free from mental slavery. I congratulate Meghraj Singh very much for writing this book.
Frankie (America)

My name is Jackie, I am Frankie's mother. Meghraj Singh is a very good person, and he has written a book "How people of the whole world will live freely." This is a very good book. Whoever reads this book will be free from mental slavery. I would like to congratulate Meghraj Singh for writing this book.

Jackie (America)

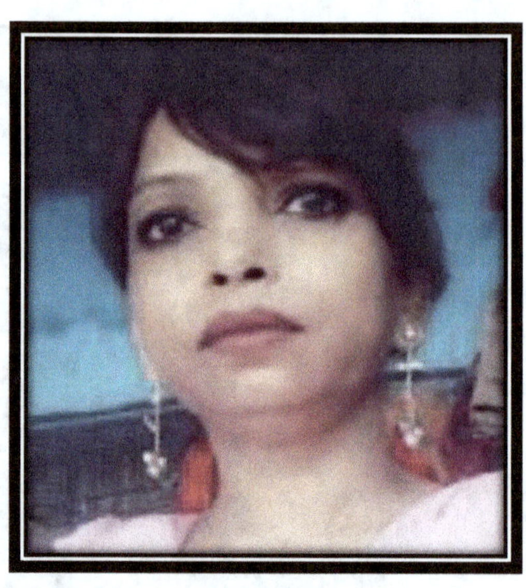

I am Manorama Chaware from Nagpur. I have known Meghraj Singh for almost two years. Meghraj Singh posts new messages on his Facebook ID every day. He is full of truth. The book written by Meghraj Singh is "How people all over the world will live a free life." This is also full of truth. Whoever reads this book will be freed from mental slavery. I congratulate Meghraj Singh for writing this book.

Manorama Chaware (Nagpur)

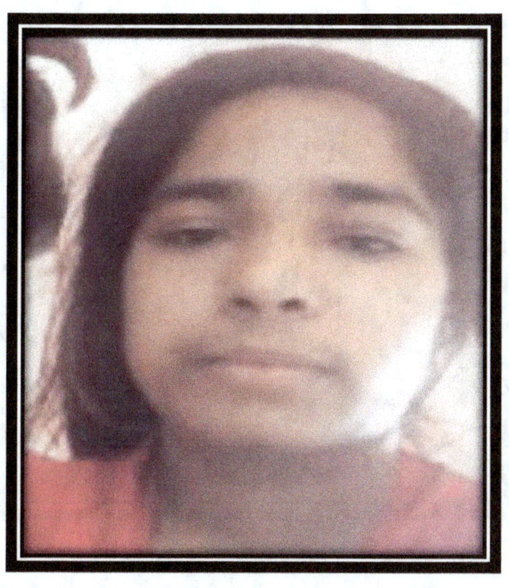

My name is Anjali Bhaskar, I am from Khushhalipur. Mental slavery is very dangerous and terrible. Whoever reads this book "How people of the whole world will live freely" will be free from mental slavery. I thank Meghraj for writing this book. I congratulate Singh very much.

Anjali Bhaskar (Khushhalipur)

My name is Santosh Sahu, I am from Chhattisgarh, I have been associated with Voice of Humanity news channel for almost two years. On this channel, there are talks about history and there are talks full of truth. The solution to avoid religious fanaticism given in the book "How humans of the whole world will live freely" written by Meghraj Singh is very beneficial. You must read this book. I congratulate Meghraj Singh for writing the book.

Santosh Sahu (Chhattisgarh)

My name is Sumit Singh, I am from Kanpur, Uttar Pradesh. Whenever I read the posts written by Meghraj Singh on Facebook, I get a lot of knowledge. After reading this book, people will get a lot of knowledge and they will all be free from mental slavery. I congratulate Meghraj Singh very much for writing this book.

Sumit Singh (Kanpur, Uttar Pradesh)

My name is Harminder Singh, I live in America. Most of the people in the world know only that there are two types of slavery, but according to me, there are many types of slavery. To understand slavery, one has to adopt the path of truth and honesty. You can correctly identify slavery by this book written by Meghraj Singh "How people of the whole world will live a life of freedom". This book will free the people of the world from mental slavery. I would like to thank Meghraj Singh for writing this book. I congratulate you very much.

Harminder Singh (America)

We have known Meghraj Singh Khalsa Gurusikh for almost four years, whatever he writes is based on truth and honesty, he is a true and good-hearted person. Only he can be a true and good-hearted person who is free from mental slavery and physical slavery. This book which has been written by Meghraj Singh ji, whose title is ~ "How humans of the whole world will live a free life", this book is very important, this book will work to bring the whole world out of mental slavery. I congratulate Meghraj Singh very much for writing this.

Swami Triptananda (India)

My name is Sarabjit Singh, I am from Yamunanagar. Mental slavery is very terrible and dangerous. Mental slavery has enslaved almost ninety percent of people in the world. This is the book written by Meghraj Singh. By reading this, people can come out of mental slavery. Meghraj Singh, read this book. I congratulate Meghraj Singh very much for writing this book.

Sarabjit Singh (Yamunanagar, India)

My name is Taranjit Kaur, I am currently a student, I have read many books in my classes, but this is a book named "How people from all over the world will live a free life" in this book I have got different knowledge after reading it, whatever this book is Those who read it will also get knowledge. I congratulate Meghraj Singh very much for writing this book.

Taranjit Kaur (India)

My name is Anita Chaudhary, I am from India. I feel that caste and caste system is the root of mental slavery. The book written by Meghraj Singh can cut this mental slavery. I congratulate Meghraj Singh for writing this book.
Anita Chaudhary (India)

I, Dr. Harpreet Kaur, when I read the book "Pure Vishva Ke Insan **Kaise Jeayenge Azadi Se Zindagi**"(How to live a life of freedom) written by Meghraj Singh, I was convinced that even today people are trapped in what kind of slavery. Whoever will read this book will, you will be able to know about the mental slavery within you and will also get information about how to get out of that slavery. I congratulate Meghraj Singh very much for writing this book.

Dr. Harpreet Kaur (Bhopal)

My name is Akalmurt Kaur, I am from Argentina. Meghraj Singh has written this book named "How people of the whole world will live a life of freedom". This is a very important book, after reading it a person can come out of slavery.
I would congratulate Meghraj Singh for writing this book.
Akalmurt Kaur (Argentina)

I am Mandeep Singh from America. I have known Meghraj Singh for about ten months. It does what it says. I have seen this very closely, the book he has written, which is called "How humans of the whole world will live their lives freely", this book will help people a lot in becoming mentally strong. You must read this book. I congratulate Meghraj very much for writing this book.
Mandeep Singh (America)

My name is Yasmin Khan, I work in Bollywood. When we look inside the world, we see people trapped in mental slavery. Meghraj Singh has written this book, whose name is "How people of the whole world will live their lives freely". The book will help people all over the world get out of mental slavery. I congratulate Meghraj Singh for writing this book.

Yasmin khan

(Model, Actor, Director in Bollywood)

My name is Raja Khan, I am a Bollywood actor. Whenever I talk to Meghraj Singh on phone, his talks are only to bring people out of mental slavery. Meghraj Singh has written this book, which is named "How people of the whole world will live a life of freedom", in this also it has shown the way out of mental slavery. Whoever reads this book will come out of mental slavery. Meghraj Singh has written this book. I congratulate you very much for writing.
Raja Khan (Bollywood Actor)

I am Officer Adil, I work in films from Mumbai. Mental slavery creates hatred in a person, creates a feeling of malice. To avoid this, it is very important to come out of mental slavery. This book written by Meghraj Singh is about mental slavery. Many things are written in it, by reading it any person can come out of slavery.

I congratulate Meghraj Singh very much for writing this book.

Afsar Adil (Bollywood Actor)

I am Zainab Brandy Bollywood Actor. I live in Mumbai, everywhere I see people hating each other and talking about killing each other, behind this I see mental slavery. Meghraj Singh has written this book, which helps people in getting rid of mental slavery. You will find a way out. I congratulate Meghraj Singh for writing this book.

Zainab Brandy (Bollywood Actor)

I am Mohammad Faisal Jani, and I am from Pakistan. Mental slavery is very dangerous. It is not an easy thing to get out of this slavery. Meghraj Singh has written the book, its name is "How people of the whole world will live a free life" This book by reading, a person can easily come out of mental slavery. I congratulate Meghraj Singh for writing this book.

Mohammad Faisal Jani (Pakistan)

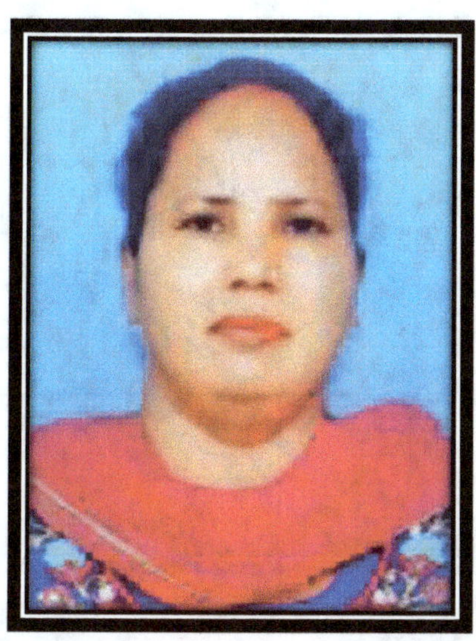

My name is Narendra Kaur, I am from Haryana. It is very difficult to identify mental slavery, and only one who can identify mental slavery can come out of it. Meghraj Singh has written this book. By reading this book, a person will become free from mental slavery. Can identify and become free from mental slavery. I congratulate Meghraj Singh very much for writing this book.
Narendra Kaur (Haryana)

The only way to live a life of freedom is to have faith in oneself and God. The person who believes in himself and has faith in God will never have to become a slave of humans.

"If a door is closed to a human being,
God opens a thousand doors for that person.
Unika Shahbaz Khan (India)

About the Author Media and Social Media

- About the Author Media and Social Media
- Former host Voice of Khalsa Radio.
- Presently director of Voice of Humanity news channel.
- Active on issues related to indigenous people and their rights on social media like Facebook, YouTube, WhatsApp, Twitter, Instagram etc.
- Poems and articles have been published in many newspapers such as Prabhat Post, Natives etc.

Song writing

I have written songs related to indigenous people and many other issues, which have been quite popular on social media. Many of these songs have been used in their respective fields, such as the film Shudra to Khalsa.

The lines of the main songs written by me are as follows: -

1. Guru Nanak Sahib Ji embraced those whom the Brahmins had degraded by calling them Shudras...!
2. Guru Gobind Singh came disguised as a male Agammada...!
3. Gurunanak Sahib respected women...!
4. We will uproot Waheguru's name regarding hypocrisy...!
5. And you fan of Bheem, please be careful...!
6. dear ones of Bhima, save the Constitution...!
7. Sikhs are brave warriors, neither afraid nor scaring anyone...!
8. There is a brave story of the mighty Sikh community...!
9. soldiers, O farmers, save your country from thieves...!
10. Come children, teach us all the lesson of truth and make our name famous in the world by serving our parents...!
11. Why should humans become enemies of humans? Let us think...!

1.) We have prepared this song in these 25 languages of the world. Such as –
2.) English
3.) Punjabi
4.) Arabic
5.) Pashtu
6.) Gujarati
7.) Rajasthani

8.) Bhojpuri

9.) Korea

10.) Afghani

11.) Persian (Farsi)

12.) Urdu

13.) Bengali

14.) Chinese

15.) Japanese

16.) Spanish

17.) French

18.) German

19.) Indonesian

20.) Nepali

21.) Turkish

22.) Romanian

23.) Italian

24.) Russian

25.) Hindi

26.) Haryanvi

12. Hypocritical babas have made India hell...!

13. We are your children, Guru, we are your children...!

14. The love between brother and sister is the sweetest in the world...!

15. Guru Nanak's Phulwadi is Sikh Sikligar...!

This song is the first international song composed on the Sikh Sikligar community.

I am the author and sponsor of this song.

The advisor of this song is Dr. Harpreet Kaur who is a Ph.D. on Sikh Sikligar community. She is the first researcher in the world to do D.

16. Transgender are also human beings, respect them all...!
17. This song is the world's first international song made on eunuchs (transgender). I am the writer of this song. The advisor of this song is knowledgeable Dharam Singh ji from Australia and the sponsor is knowledgeable Makhan Singh ji from Australia.
18. Thanks to Guru Gobind Singh Ji...!
19. This is the mission of great men which we are carrying out...!
20. Saint Ravidas ji was born on the land of Banaras...!
21. Whenever true friends have taken steps together...!
22. Truth is our life; truth is our pride...!
23. As Salaam Valekum Salaam Gift for all the world Muslim community...!
24. Live with love, loving creatures...! (Gift for Pradeep Kaur)
25. New enthusiasm, new wave, move in a new direction...! (Gipt for Taranjeer Kaur)
26. Wake up, natives, take charge of your own rule...!
27. With Voice Humanity News Channel, we will spread the truth to the whole world...!
28. Those who ask for dowry are the biggest beggars...!

29. Mind is the form of God; mind is the form of Satan...!
30. We have come alone; we will go alone...!
31. Youth of the world, make your future successful...!
32. Wake up youth, she is the one to enter politics...! (Qawwali) (song)
33. This is a unique gender; they also need respect...!

There are four books written by me whose names are as follows...

1.) Is Sikh Hindu? Know what is the truth.
2.) Truth is religion.
3.) What is the solution to the serious problems of families and the world? (Come know)
4.) How will humans all over the world live a life of freedom? (Come let's know)

ਬਾਣੀ ਗੁਰੂ ਗੁਰੂ ਹੈ ਬਾਣੀ ਵਿਚਿ ਬਾਣੀ
ਗੁਰੂ ਬਾਣੀ ਕਹੈ ਸੇਵਕੁ ਜਨੁ ਮਾਨੈ ਪਰਤਖਿ
Guroo Naanak Sikh Sabh

For example, if we sow a seed inside the earth, the earth will grow into a tree and bear many times more fruits. Similarly, the mind is also like an earth. If you sow lies or truth in the mind, then the earth in the form of mind will also give its fruits many times more.

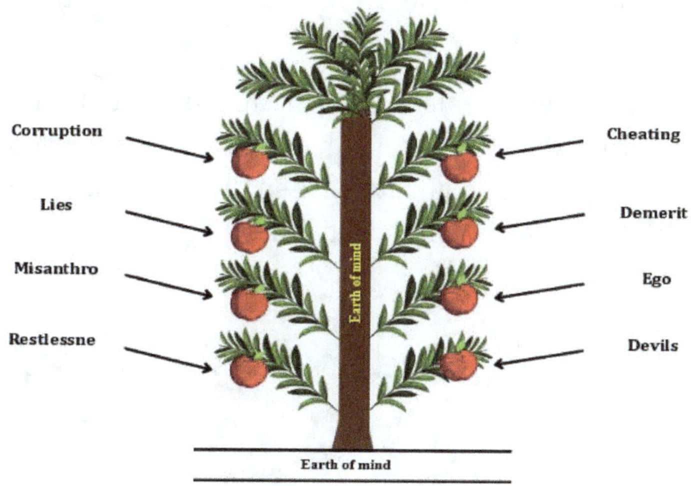

Earth of mind

- Corruption

- Lies

- Misanthrope

- Restlessness

- Cheating

- Demerit

- Ego

- Devils

What fruit will we get from the seeds of lies from the earth of mind?

If you sow the seed of lie in the earth of the mind, the mind will grow into a tree and bear the fruits of dishonesty, oppression, misconduct, rape, hatred and devilry.

The mind will remain restless all the time. O restless mind, it will fill the body with hatred from within and will eat away the good qualities. Then the mind will give only sorrow to the person throughout his life.

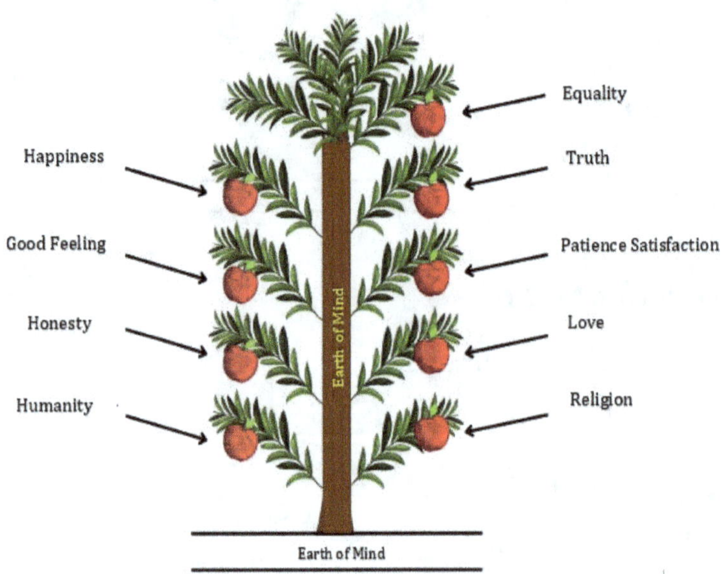

Earth of mind

- Happiness
- good feeling
- Honesty

- humanity

- Equality

- Truth

- patience satisfaction

- Love

- religion

What fruit will we get from the earth of mind and the truth?

If we sow the seed of truth in the earth of the mind, the mind will grow into a tree and bear the fruits of truth, honesty, patience, contentment, equality, humanity and love.

In happiness and sorrow, the mind will keep a person strong and will save him from hatred, then the mind will give only happiness to the person throughout his life.

Note - A true and honest person can neither become a mental slave nor can he suffer from mental diseases. He will always live a life of freedom and will teach others to live a life of freedom too.